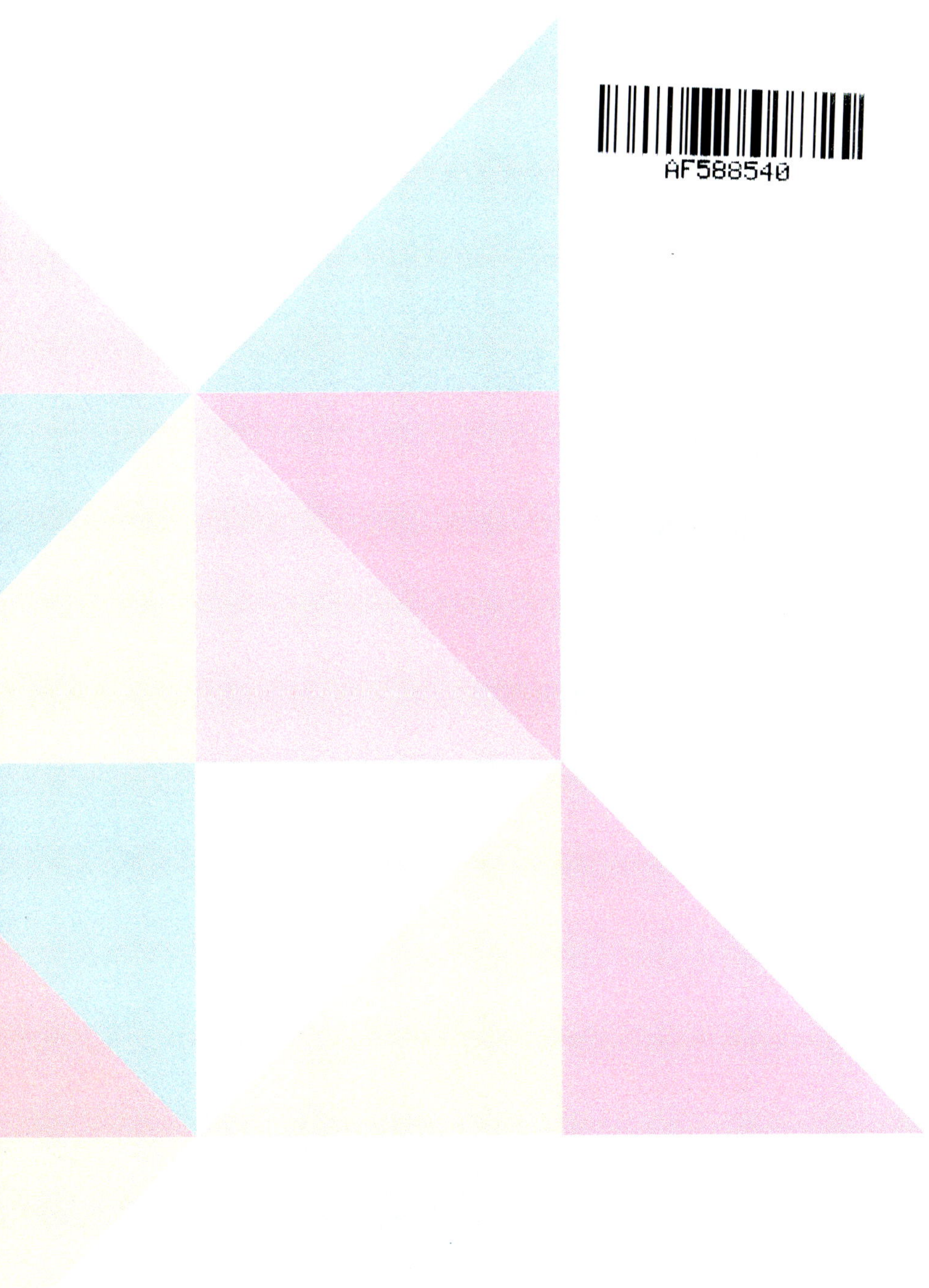

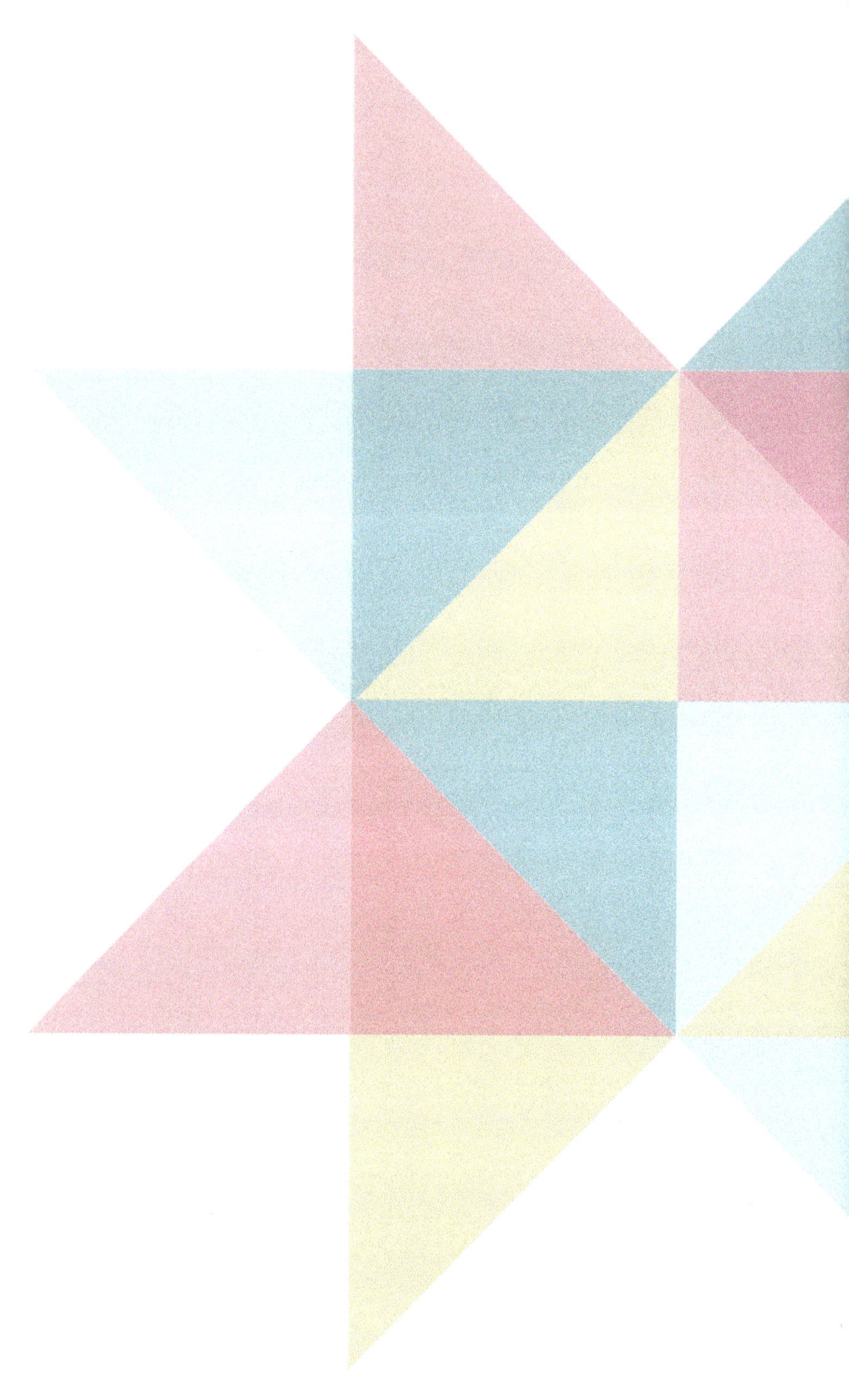

WORKSHOPS UNLEASHED

How to Design Engaging and Successful Workshops for Quilters and Crafters

By Tori McElwain

Visit the author's website at TheQuiltPatchbyTori.com.

For information about special discounts available for bulk purchases, sales promotions, fund-raising, and educational needs, contact The Quilt Patch by Tori at hello@thequiltpatchbytori.com.

Copyediting by Melissa Strange
Book Cover by Tori McElwain, Kathleen Fritzsche, and Sarah Hall
Illustrations by Tori McElwain, with photography contributions by Sarah Hall and Darla Hall

Library of Congress Control Number: 2024920148
IBSN 9798218482183
1st edition September 2024

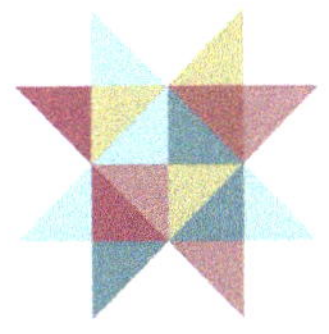

This book is dedicated to my kids.

If I can do it, you can do it too.

Contents

Section One

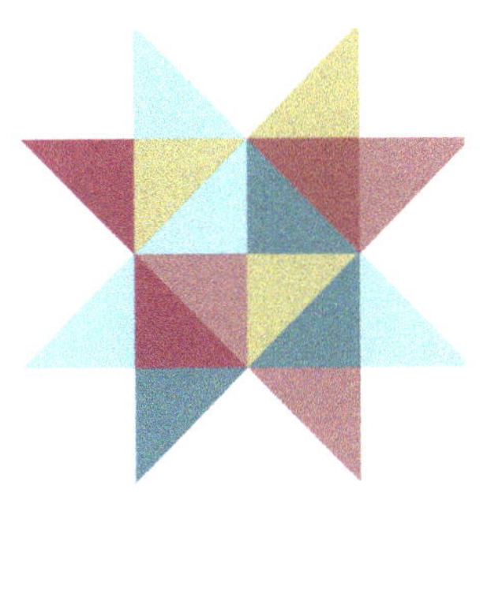

Introduction

How to Use This Book

You can use this book to design any learning experience: classes, courses, workshops, craft-a-longs, summits, webinars, trainings, masterclasses, or workshops—online and in person. It provides the tools, resources, and marketing you need to help you design a wonderful learning experience.

You can choose to read it cover-to-cover or skip around to different sections as you need them.

- Write in the margins
- Highlight favorite parts of the book
- Note your answers
- Use as your curriculum planner
- Go through what you need or read it from cover to cover

I encourage you to treat this book as a workbook and reference that can stay home or travel with you.

You can download PDFs of templates, worksheets for the exercises, and the Curriculum Map for your workshop through the provided QR code in the Resources section. See you there!

The Road to *Workshops Unleashed*

I sat very still, in shock, as he droned on, much like the adult voices in a Charlie Brown cartoon. It was two weeks after our wedding and his idea would change everything. Every plan, choice, and strategy I had put into place for my life would have to change.

I'm a person who likes a plan. It doesn't have to be full of detail, but general guidelines guide and comfort me through this crazy thing called life, and here is my new husband proposing the idea of joining the military.

"But it's not what you think! I'd be an officer after training is done," he explained.

He had no idea what I was thinking.

That conversation was a turning point. It felt like my life had been thrown into turmoil, and I was standing still in the middle, watching the world turn around me. I finished my bachelor's degree in history and child development, graduated, and two months later packed up my little brown Ford Tracer, threw our dog in the back, and drove from California to Georgia to be with my new husband. At that point, we had spent five months together out of our first year of marriage.

I spent my time in Georgia in a blind routine. I didn't know what to do with myself. Ideas would pop up and I'd make excuses, ignoring the dread of being useless that was growing in the back of my mind.

One thing I did try to do was make friends, and I bet if you've been a stay-at-home spouse you may guess what happened next—I got pulled into an MLM (Multi-Level Marketing). In short, the company was awful, but it gave me the first spark of entrepreneurship. I was finally inspired to invent my future. If I couldn't follow my original plan, I'd create a new one.

What did I want to do? Teach! I've always wanted to teach. From Girl Scouts to dance to leadership in high school and college—everything I enjoyed revolved around teaching. I did the research and prepared for our first duty station in Texas. We were there for almost four years. I worked hard earning a Texas teaching certificate and Master's in Curriculum and Instruction at the same time. I worked full-time as an aide and then two years as a Kindergarten teacher before my life got flipped upside down yet again.

This flip came in the form of a tiny human. One that stole my heart and shifted all my priorities. My son was born a week after the school year ended and three months before we moved (again). We arrived in South Carolina at the end of the summer. I was a new mom, a burned-out teacher, and had no idea when or where we were heading after our short station in South Carolina. I had no desire to return to the classroom. The spark of entrepreneurship that I'd felt four years prior was still sparkling in the back of my mind, and I wondered, "Could this spark turn into more?"

I used my hobby for inspiration and sold quilts and baby blankets. I pivoted after almost a year to a more scalable endeavor: Quilt Pattern Design and teaching workshops. I always seemed to be pulled back to teaching. Within this space of pattern design and workshop development, I traveled around the country both in person and virtually to present at Quilt Guilds. I soon found myself again creatively burned out and knew that this wasn't quite what I needed.

I pivoted again to teaching the teacher. I saw this gap both in the quilting industry, in my military spouse community, and even in my family where women were being told to do more and charge less. They were told that they weren't worthy without a degree—their time and experience meant nothing. On the flip side, I also saw amazingly creative women wanting to teach but not being confident enough to start. These very creative women also had a trend of being able to demonstrate what they did but not being able to transfer their skills efficiently. In other words, they could make beautiful things and wanted to help others but were not able to teach their skills in a comprehensive way and in the time allotted.

I felt called to help change that narrative and it became concrete on the day that Darla Hall reached out to me for help. Darla Hall was an award-winning longarm, free motion quilter when she approached me about teaching workshops in person and online. We went over everything she would need to create: her curriculum, class structure, landing pages, setting up a Zoom account, and equipment. We even discussed pricing, ensuring she was fairly compensated for her skill, experience, and time.

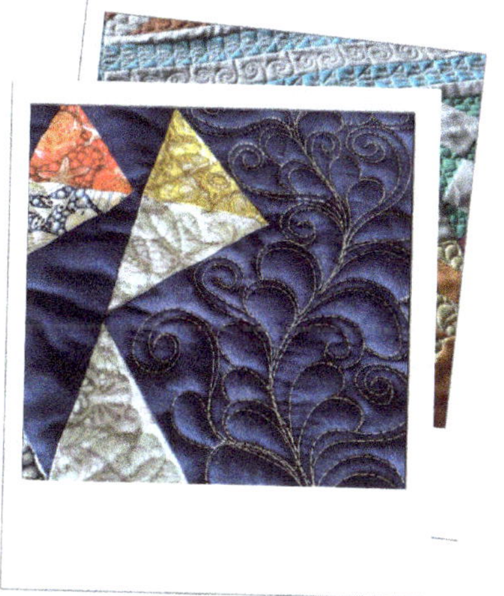

Just like Darla, your time and experience are extremely valuable. Your expertise is wanted and *needed*. Your call to teach is a beautiful sign; let's unleash your creativity and help others release theirs. Workshops transfer skills and knowledge. Our skills as quilters and crafters are creative skills that are desperately needed in this tech-driven world. Creativity is essential for humans. Creativity makes space for problem-solving, improving memory, and creating joy and fun! Workshops are an amazing way to give that away. I invite you to use this book to unleash your creativity and help spread joy, fun, and creativity around the world.

Imagine if one person in every community decided to create and teach a workshop. They teach six people, then those six people in turn teach six people, and so on and so forth, creating a ripple that unleashes creativity and joy in a world that desperately needs it. Let's get started unleashing your workshop.

Set up Intentional Time to Focus on Your Goals

There are so many activities to do in a day. For many of us, it's a never-ending task list that grows and grows with fun, challenging, and mundane tasks that all seem to have some semblance of high priority or urgency. However, to create an engaging and successful workshop, you need to take action. You will need to write out the exercises laid out in the following sections and write down your thoughts and notes as you read—that takes time.

I don't mean setting time aside or finding the time somewhere in your schedule. If you want your workshop to be successful, you need to carve out time to make it happen. This book was written to help you design and plan a successful workshop from start to finish, but you will need to put the plan into action when the time comes to share and teach.

One of the largest barriers to moving a plan to action is time. Let's get **focused** and intentional with focus time.

Carving Time Out

It's time to grab your calendar and make a plan. Tell key people about it, especially those that will assist you and encourage you.

Then stick to it. Protect that time.

Take stock of your time. How do you typically spend your time during the week? When do you have the energy to dedicate time to your workshop?

Look for gaps in your week where you can dedicate focused time. This can look like two hours after breakfast where you can sit, read, plan, and still have the energy to sew or create in the afternoon. This can look like an hour each day after the kids go to bed or before they wake up. It could be a block of four hours on a weekend morning when you agree to switch babysitting duties with a neighbor, sister, brother, or friend. It could be a Thursday evening where Thursdays are your "do not disturb" days. Maybe you take an extra-long lunch on Fridays or block out time on Monday mornings.

Make the time, then protect it. Block it out in your calendar and tell your assistant, your partner, and even your kids or grandkids that you will be unreachable (or just busy) during that time.

Then, here's the toughest part, enforce it.

Do not answer the phone, texts, or emails. Lock the door to the office, put up a curtain, or hunker down in a closet (I see you toddler mom. I was you!) and separate yourself so that you can focus and be very intentional with your time. As a mom and a recovering people pleaser, I know how hard this can be. But knowing that you've read this far, you need this focus time. So, enforce it!

Create a Goal for this Dedicated Time

When you have your time blocked out, it's time to create a goal or objective, or several. This can be as formal as you'd like it to be. Just state it to yourself or create measurable objectives.

Your goal or objective for this time should fit into one sentence. It should be clear, concise, and measurable with a number or with a yes or no answer.

Example 1: I want to learn to sew by taking "X" course and making a shirt! Did you do it? Yes or no? This answer is clear and tangible.

Example 2: I will complete the introduction to *Workshops Unleashed* during my Focus Time today (hey, you're almost there!). Did you complete it? Yes or No?

As I mentioned above, setting these goals and objectives can be formal (write it out!) or informal (keep it in your mind). Writing down a goal or objective can be very powerful, but so can keeping that goal or objective to yourself. Whichever motivates you to stick to your *Focus Time* is the route I would suggest you take.

One last thing: *be gentle with yourself.* You're human. If you don't make your objective or hit your goal every time or in a perfect way—it's OKAY. Adjust your goal or your plan to make the goal *enjoyable, achievable, and manageable.*

Plan It Out

I'm a strategist. It's part of what I love to do.

Certain sections of this book, as well as activities and prep work for your workshop, will need more planning than just a single objective. My favorite strategy to suggest for others who have multiple steps in a project or process is similar to an ongoing list.

If you need assistance in planning, here are three steps to get you started:

Step 1: Make a list. A long one. List everything (and I mean everything!) you'd want to do.

Step 2: Go back and circle 1–3 things that you can realistically do during your Focus Time and excite you the most (go with your gut!) and *meet your objective(s).*

Step 3: List out the next three action steps you need to take to get started.

Why three? So many reasons, but I'll keep it short:

- Three is easy to remember
- Three action steps make a task more doable
- Three helps you make progress and it *feels* good
- Quick wins create momentum
- Three likely helps you hit three weeks. Creating a new habit (like giving yourself intentional focus time) takes twenty-one days or three weeks.

Step 4: Write it on the calendar!

You've made the time, now attach an action step to that time! This can be by day on a written calendar, or a digital one on the phone, or week by week (i.e. Week One: do this; Week Two: do this next).

Revisit steps 2–4 as you complete your action steps.

Example Action Steps 1: I will make my *Target the Stars* quilt in five weeks to have a sample for the workshop. Next week, I will pick my fabric and start cutting. In week two, I will have all my fabric cut and the first four quilt blocks sewn together. During week three, I will finish the top and write out the next three weeks based on my progress and the pattern.

Example Action Steps 2: I will create the workshop for my *Target the Stars* quilt pattern. On day one, I will map the workshop. On day two, I will write out the details I want to add that are not in the pattern. On day three, I will pick the fabric palette and share it on social media with a teaser and outline my script.

That's nice, Tori, but I want to do many different things!

If that sounds like you, try to choose themes for time blocks.

For instance, if you've chosen a daily time block for learning from this book.

Day 1–2 can be reading.

Day 3 is for applying what you're learning.

Day 4 is meeting with an accountability partner.

Day 5 is extra. Need more time to implement? Need to clean up your notes or organize your space? Want to keep reading or researching outside of this book? Use this day!
Let's get to it and start achieving those goals!

Increase the Focus

I'm sure you've seen advice on how to help yourself focus before. I'm going to reiterate what has worked best for me. Try a few things out and figure out what works for you!

1. "Silence" the phone. This can be literally with "Do Not Disturb," but this works best for me when I just leave it in a different room or put something on top of my phone so it's out of sight, but I can still hear it if I need to.

2. White noise, music, or a podcast.

3. Drink water and eat a snack that makes you feel energized before you get started.

4. Have a designated spot (i.e., under a tree in your backyard, the closet, the basement, the kitchen table, or your own room) for your focus time, if possible.

Creating an environment that allows you to focus is important. Once you find a rhythm, whatever that looks like to you, it will help you get in the zone for your Focus Time.

I used to live in a one-bedroom apartment with my husband when he first joined the military. There was no kitchen table. We had a little counter off the kitchen and a coffee table. This is when I started quilting again using the yardage and scraps my mom had given me that didn't fit her palette anymore.

I would turn on the news, fill my water, and set up my little Brother sewing machine on the coffee table. Doing these three things each time I started to quilt got my mind ready to quilt. It helped set the tone that it was time to create! Then I would pack it up and store the machine and fabric in the corner of the room when the time was done—signaling to my brain that it was time to switch gears.

Creating a rhythm and changing your environment can help you focus to accomplish your goal on time.

Planning & Slipping

Don't forget to make your focus time fulfilling and energizing. If it's not fulfilling and energizing (like structured playtime!), it's less likely that you will continue. You will find yourself slipping back to emptying your cup without creating that time to refill it.

Speaking of slipping…you can slip and restart. Seriously, it will be okay. If your focus time takes a backseat for a few weeks or months and you find yourself needing that time again, start the process over. Every season of life brings new challenges and, realistically, your focus time may be hard to enforce when you have a newborn or you're taking care of an aging parent, starting a new job, getting major surgery, or getting a puppy. Focus time should be serving you, not draining you.

When you're ready to start again, possibly start smaller. What do you need now? It could look different, which is a beautiful part of being human. We grow, we change, we learn, and we can relearn.

One more time just in case you skimmed: We grow, we change, we learn, and we ***can*** *relearn!*

One more important piece of advice before we get started—write.

Write It Out

Are you lost in the weeds? Do you have so many thoughts, projects, and even class and course ideas in the works at all times?

If you need clarity or organization, write it out.

When I decided to shift my business from making handmade quilts to designing quilt patterns and workshops, my imagination went wild for the someday that could come. I envisioned my patterns hanging in quilt shops and vending at QuiltCon and the International Quilt Festival in Houston, Texas. I had so many ideas for workshops and courses that I wanted to create and educate my fellow quilters—I was just full and brimming with ideas. This rush of ideas slowed me down. I had so many ideas that I couldn't focus.

One of the best pieces of advice I received was to create a "Some Day, Maybe List." Grab a journal or a notebook and write all your ideas down that you want to make happen someday, just not *today*.

I'm not so organized that I have one journal for this purpose, but I have a host of notebooks around my sewing room that I use to jot ideas down. I sketch quilt ideas, take notes from classes I've taken, and note down all the ideas that are sparked by listening to podcasts. This helps get them out of my head and onto paper—a permanent place where I won't lose the idea. This freed up so much space in my brain! I was able to choose what I was most excited about and could reasonably make happen and worked on those first.

I have heard others refer to a similar practice under many different names. Throughout this book, I use the term *brainstorm*—writing down all the information your brain has and getting it out on paper. This will help you see all the ideas in one place, make space in your thoughts for the most important and pressing work at hand, and will help you organize those thoughts, steps, or ideas in order and in bite-sized steps to tackle your next goal.

Since you have this book in hand, I assume one of those goals is to create a workshop, so let's get started!

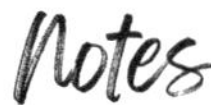

"There are people in this world that will never become their best until you become your best"

\- **Earl Nightingale**

Section Two

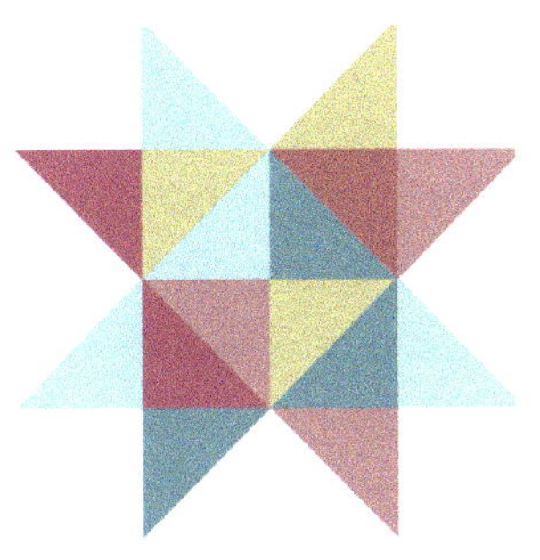

Design Your Workshop

I Have No Idea What to Teach: An Exercise

The first step to teaching a workshop is to identify the kind of workshop you want to create. If you've picked this book, I am assuming you have the drive, the want, and the desire to teach. However, that doesn't mean you know exactly what you want to teach. My experience has taught me that quilting and crafting teachers either know exactly what they want to teach, and it's very niche-specific, or they default to teaching basics. Take a few moments to truly consider what you want to teach with the exercise below.

When choosing a process, pattern, or skill to teach, it's important to consider not only what you're knowledgeable about in your craft but also what you *truly* enjoy teaching. What I have found beneficial is to brainstorm.

The Brainstorm!

This can be done on a sheet of paper or with Post-its!

Reflect on projects showcasing the skills you have mastered *and* have enjoyed doing even if you may not be considering teaching. What are some skills that people have commented on or asked if you could show them how to do? You may even have had people ask you to teach them a skill or pattern in particular. Write all of it down. Consider all the skills within your craft, and also explore skills *outside* your craft that could be integrated into your class.

Note any ideas that come up and add them to your brainstorm. Are you tech-savvy? Add that. Do you love another hobby or craft that is influencing this craft? Write that down. Love cars? Write that down. Love gardening? Write that down. Love architecture, math, spreadsheets, and organizing? Write it all down.

If you're struggling or having a hard time putting words to these skills, reach out to friends or family and ask them what your strengths are. See what they think you're good at and see if that lines up with what you have written down. Another helpful tool is taking a personality strengths test. There are many to choose from and some are even free online. One example I've used is the CliftonStrengths or Strengths Finder assessment. You may have already taken one for an organization. Take a look at what that assessment has determined and write those down as well.

Now that you have written down all your skills and ideas on paper, take a look at your skills and note how they can be connected. Look for *themes* between the listed items. What can be grouped together? Are many of your projects pointing to a particular technique? Does this generate new ideas for future workshops? Or maybe this process is validating your current workshop idea. Does this list pull you away from the workshops you already teach? Can you create a unique workshop using your skills?

If you're unsure, sit with this list for a few days and let the ideas "cook" in the back of your mind.

Next step, circle what excites you! Then, narrow it down to 1–3 topics or workshop ideas. Ideally, there is one that stands out. If you have more than one, pick three that you are most enthusiastic about. Take that workshop idea to the next section and write a clear objective!

How do you only pick one workshop?

As creatives, we tend to be multi-passionate individuals. We love so many things about our craft that it can be hard to narrow that down to one subject to create a workshop around.

I used to feel so much pressure to start with basics or start with the technique I've done the longest, but my best advice is to think long-term and about what lights you up.

Take some time to think about the answers to the following questions:

- What excites you the most? What lights you up?
- What could you do or talk about all day long?
- What do you want to be known for?

Also, check in with your energy level when you're considering which workshop topic to choose. You want to choose a topic that fuels you, gives you energy, and is easy to talk about. Not one that you're feeling obligated or expected to teach. You want to feel confident and excited about adding to the conversation on your topic. You also want to make sure you are ready to hold onto this topic for the long term.

I had a client meet with me to help her narrow this choice down. She was a Judy Niemeyer Certified Instructor and has taught Judy Niemeyer patterns for a long time. These patterns are large with many pieces and are designed to be a labor of love with show-stopping beauty. I recalled her detailing how she "could teach it in her sleep." The advice she received was to start her business with Judy Niemeyer Workshops, sell her fabric as she had, and then build up her longarming business in her new location after that.

You should have seen her. This wonderfully talented woman has gone through some serious life changes. She looked almost devastated while telling me this. It was plain to me that as her current circumstances changed; her passion for teaching Judy Niemeyer patterns did not follow her. My question for her was, “What is one thing you are most excited about?” And you should have seen her transformation. She sat up straight, a big smile spread across her face as she told me about her longarming business. When I pointed out how her body language had just shifted and her tone lit up with feeling, it clicked for her that longarming was where her heart was. My next question was, “What do you want to be known for?” She spoke about all the different things she had for sale: patterns, fabric, workshops, and longarming services (again with that unconscious excitement!). I had to gently interrupt and ask again, “What do you want to be known for?”

She paused and determinedly answered “Longarming. But what do I do with all this other stuff?”

I’m going to give you the same advice I gave her. If you want to be known as THE longarmer, or THE color teacher, or THE Irish chain expert, drop the other “stuff” and dive in deep with what you want to be known for. Tula Pink does many things, but the one thing she is known for is being a modern fabric designer. That is where Tula Pink dived in deep and that is what she’s most known for. Judy Niemeyer is THE show-stopping, medallion-style quilt pattern designer; Karley Porter is THE Graffiti Quilter; Annie of ByAnnie is THE quilted bag designer. If you want to be known for it—go all in.

If you're a multi-passionate creative who is tempted to design a workshop around all the things you love to do, my advice is to start with what excites you the most. If they all excite you and you can't possibly choose, what is the easiest or simplest workshop you can design now? Start teaching, inviting students in and getting feedback, and then start teaching what your audience is craving or inspired to learn.

One thing that stopped me from going all in was the fear of burnout or boredom. If it's burnout you're worried about, take breaks and hold firm boundaries as we discussed in the Focus Time section. If it's boredom, you can change the thing you're known for—just bring your audience with you! Elizabeth Chappell of Quilters Candy is a beautiful example. She began her business selling boxes of notions and fabric and wonderful quilty items to quilters. She pivoted her business to a membership of modern quilt patterns, then to fabric design. She also started coaching other quilting and crafting businesses. She built respect, authority, and revenue by going all in on one thing as it came to her and gracefully pivoted as her interests pivoted.

Clarity is Essential: Write an Objective

Congratulations! Whether you already knew your topic or have narrowed it down, I want to take a moment to applaud you. You have taken another large step forward in creating your next workshop!

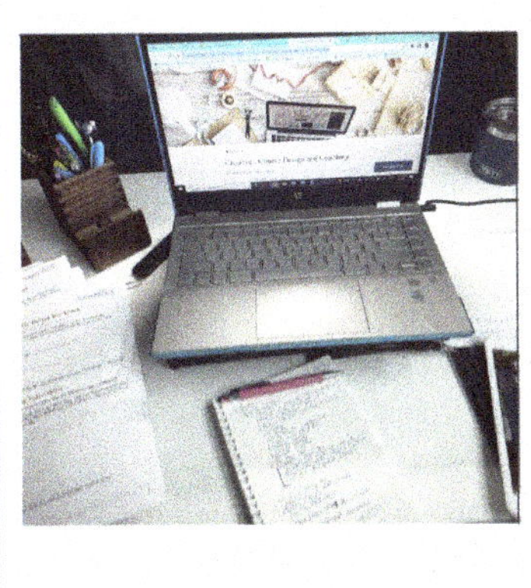

Your next step is to create an objective. This step is essential to ensure you are clear on what you're teaching and communicating to your future students.

What you're teaching should fit into one sentence. It should be clear, concise, and measurable with a yes or no. This is all about clear communication. If you can describe the workshop clearly in one sentence, you can communicate your goal (which is also their goal!) to your students. Also, avoid using "I" or the first person. The objective and ultimately the description that you can use for your workshop should be centered on the student.

To add clarity and interest to your workshop description, your objective should have an action verb. What action or actions are your students performing in the workshop? I'm sure you've most likely seen the phrase "in this workshop we will be..." or the phrase "the objective of the workshop is..." Both of these phrases are fine to use, but they don't capture the kind of attention we want to bring to your workshop. You want to avoid using them in your workshop description and instead work on that action verb. Let's work backward from those two common phrases to create a working objective that we can use later in our description.

When asked what the objective of the workshop is, many instructors will begin by saying, "The objective of this workshop is..." To keep it more concise, begin with, "This workshop is..."

Our working objective now reads, "*This workshop is to teach beginners how to piece a top.*"

First, add the name of the workshop and think about who your audience is. Then, add in who you are speaking to. In this example, it's beginner *quilters*. So, our working objective would read like this, "*Quilting 101 is to teach beginner quilters how to piece a top.*"

Second, add an action verb and remove the phrase, "is to teach." (This phrase is all about the teacher—we want this objective to be student-focused.) What specific action(s) are the students in the workshop performing? At this point, a list may be useful. In a beginner quilting workshop, a beginner quilter could perform the following actions (remember to be specific!):

- cutting with rotary tools
- measuring accurately
- sewing a ¼ seam
- lining up pieces or nesting seams accurately
- pressing

- ripping out stitches

From this list, you will take the skills you most want them to learn. For this example, I am using cutting efficiently, sewing a ¼ seam, and nesting seams. Then, add these skills to the working objective. By shifting the tense a bit and adding a few descriptive words to help the skills fit in, our working objective now reads as, "*In Quilting 101, beginner quilters will learn to cut efficiently, sew a ¼-inch seam, and learn how to nest their seams for beautiful and accurate piecing to piece a top.*"

What an improvement! Now, the cherry on top—the project! What are they making? How will students show how they have demonstrated the skills listed above? What fun and beginner-friendly project will you have them make? My go-to is either a pillowcase or a table runner. After including the project in our sentence, our objective now reads, "*In Quilting 101, beginner quilters will learn to cut efficiently, sew a ¼-inch seam, and learn how to nest their seams for beautiful and accurate piecing while creating a classic Friendship Star Pillowcase!*"

The final step is to read it out loud. Is it clear? Concise? Adjust as needed! This step-by-step guide will give you a great start. Now, you have a clear direction and focus for your workshop and a great starting description for marketing!

The Role of an Objective in Marketing: Clarity in the Sparkle and Spice

With the clear, concise, and measurable objective created for the workshop, you can now use this objective when calling your people to your workshop (a.k.a. your marketing)! It creates clarity and sets expectations of what the students will be doing, however, we can add some sparkle to entice your future students.

You can spice it up a little or use it word for word. For example, here is a clear and concise objective: "*Learners will piece together half-square triangle blocks, using the two-at-a-time method, to create the Star-Studded Pillowcase.*" This can be spiced up by adding in some descriptive language: "*Learn how to create the beautiful Star-Studded Pillowcase using the beginner-friendly, two-at-a-time half-square triangle method!*" Using the objective as the basis for the description allows you to add color and fun without losing clarity.

Spice up your description by adding an answer to your students' challenge or frustration. Having a clear objective can help you identify these frustrations, challenges, or pain points, and address how you have the answer to these frustrations in your workshop. For example, in a quilted pillow workshop, a challenge a potential learner might face is attaching the zipper (I think I just felt many quilters shudder at the word zipper), but it's okay! You have added to your description that you have a *"simple and easy way to install the zipper to finish off this beautiful project!"*

Putting this all together, your description for your workshop could sound like this: "*Learn how to create the beautiful Star-Studded Pillowcase using the beginner-friendly, two-at-a-time half-square triangle method! Have you ever installed a zipper before? Learn a simple and easy way to install the zipper to finish off this beautiful project. Join me, this Saturday, for a fun afternoon of sewing and learning!"*

Or without a question:

Learn how to create the beautiful Star-Studded Pillowcase using the beginner-friendly, two-at-a-time half-square triangle method! Learn a simple and easy way to install the zipper to finish off this beautiful project. Join me, this Saturday, for a fun afternoon of sewing and learning!

The description above is fun and clear and addresses the biggest challenge we identified. Sounds like a fun workshop. Sign me up!

It's your turn to add your sparkle or spice.

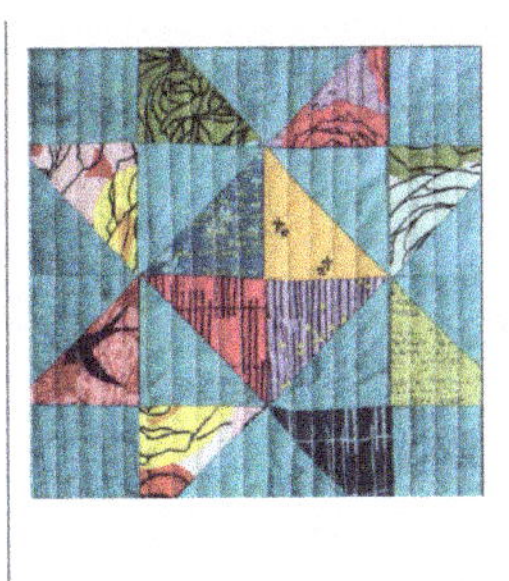

The overall goal is to be sure your objective can clearly answer the following questions. What is the objective of the course? What will the students be able to do after the workshop? The exercise below is a great way to brainstorm ideas. Write everything that comes to mind (especially for questions 2–4) in short phrases or words. The following exercise is meant to be a brain dump so that you have a bank of phrases or words to choose from.

Let's write out a few phrases, sentences, or words for the next few questions:

- What are your future students doing before looking for the workshop?

- How are they feeling now before the workshop?
- What are they doing in the workshop that will solve the challenges and frustrations they are facing?
- What can they do after they complete your workshop? How will they feel after the workshop?

You can go deeper into emotion as well:

How are they feeling about ____[topic] before your workshop?

How do they feel after your workshop about _____ [topic]?

What you want to do here is illustrate a transformation or a problem to a solution. The contrast between how your learners feel before the workshop and how they will feel after the workshop illustrates the result in a very powerful way.

Many instructors get caught up in only sharing the project that they are creating in the workshop, although that is interesting, what can be more powerful and help your future students choose you over another instructor is specifically looking at how our learners will feel or what skills they will be gaining, not the end project they've created.

Let's say, I love to make quilts with raw edge appliqué (because I do!) and want to teach other quilters the fun they could have with the raw edge appliqué technique.

First, identify who your students are. For this example, I would be reaching out to quilters who haven't tried raw edge appliqué successfully before. Then, answer the questions below.

Question 1: What is the objective of the workshop?

Quilters will sew a simple raw edge appliquéd block that they create from a simple silhouette. (If you need help with a clear, concise, and measurable objective, check out the Objective section.)

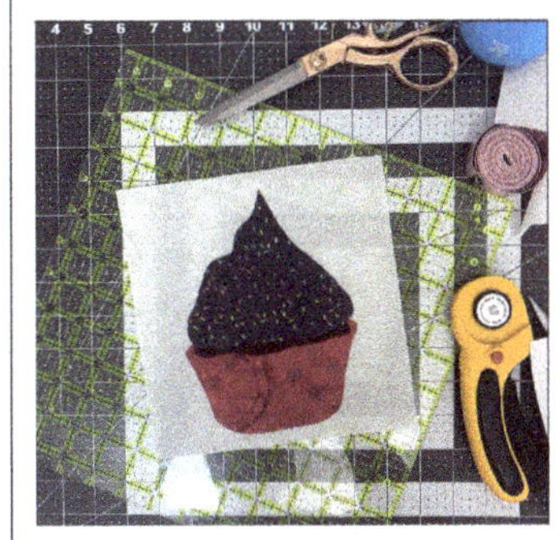

Question 2: What are your students doing before looking for the workshop?

They are admiring appliquéd quilts and are intimidated to start. They have an idea or project in mind that they want to create but are stuck on technicalities such as which stabilizer to use or what thread. They have watched 100 YouTube videos but can't seem to make their appliqué lay flat. They see patterns that mention appliqué, but they have no idea what that means.

Question 3: How are they feeling now before the workshop?

They are quilting with traditional piecing and feel limited in what they can create. They have an idea in their mind of projects they'd like to create but have no idea how to make them. They see raw edge appliqué patterns that they'd like to create but feel intimidated. They are lost, overwhelmed, frustrated, confused, or feeling like they just can’t get it right.

Question 4: What are they doing in the workshop that will solve the challenges and frustrations they are facing?

Quilters will be able to recreate a raw edge appliqué project from simple silhouettes. They will learn about thread options, the most common stabilizers, and how to secure their appliqué so it lays correctly. They will be able to follow future raw edge appliqué patterns with much more ease.

Question 5: What can they do after they complete the workshop? How will they feel after the workshop?

They will be able to make quilt blocks with raw edge appliqué. They will know which stabilizer to use, how to secure the edges, how to ensure it lays flat, and be able to create their silhouettes or basic patterns if they choose to. They will be open to being more creative in their quilt-making. They will feel accomplished in learning a new skill and excited to learn what else they can create with raw edge appliqué. They could also feel empowered and ready to dive into more advanced raw edge appliqué techniques and patterns.

Woah! That was a lot! Look at all the emotions and descriptions you can pull to create a description for your workshop. For formatting purposes, I stuck with sentences, but you may have lists of words that illustrate these emotions and descriptions. You do NOT have to use everything, but let's try and pull a few words or phrases from each question.

Your description could look something like this:

"The creative possibilities of Raw Edge Appliqué can help make your project ideas come to life! In my Introductory Raw Edge Appliqué Workshop, you can go from feeling stuck with traditional piecing to feeling prepared, creative, and empowered. In this introductory workshop, we will be making a raw edge appliquéd block that you create from a simple silhouette. You can turn this quilt block into a mat, pillow, or wall hanging—it's up to you!"

Side Note

Whenever I do this exercise, my objective tends to shift or sometimes completely change—that is okay. We called it a "working objective" because it can change with the needs, wants, emotions, or projects you decide to include with your description as you move through more detailed exercises.

Not too shabby! We shared the transformation, the objective, what they will be doing, how they will be able to use the project, and how they can use raw edge appliqué as a skill in the future. It's a great description to start with! You can always tweak it later.

The most important thing is to start. It's much easier to edit a description you have than to create a new one!

What if you have no idea how the audience you're trying to reach feels or what they are stuck on? Keep it simple and reach out to them. Find a crafter friend, acquaintance, or even a Facebook group and ask, "What is your biggest struggle with ____[topic]?" Try to find three people (or one large group) that are very similar to the audience you want to teach. This will give you valuable insight into struggles you may not have thought of, as well as phrases and words to use in marketing your workshop.

As you prepare for your workshop, take a few minutes to follow the process outlined below to help create a compelling workshop description that is clear, transformative, sparkly, and spicy.

Step 1: Write out a clear, concise, and measurable objective.

Step 2: Add some sparkle with descriptive words.

Step 3: Add some spice: Name 2–3 challenges or pain points your learners might think of when they see your description by pulling from your brain dump from questions two and three.

Step 4: Add the solutions you have listed in questions four and five to address the challenge or the pain points and add them to your description.

Step 5: Put it all together and read it out loud. Adjust for grammar and clarity.

This exercise will set your workshop up with a beautiful description and help you plan it efficiently while providing clarity, a sense of transformation, and excitement to call your learners into your workshop!

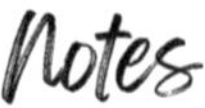

"if you're waiting until you're ready, you've already waited too long"
- **James Wedmoore**

Designing Your Workshop: Map It Out!

A Curriculum Map is where you lay out your workshop's objective, steps, key points of teaching, materials, and any other important information. Mapping out your workshop is an excellent way to organize the information and process you'll be sharing. The Curriculum Map is designed to be flexible, allowing you to move around as needed. For example, you might find it easier to plan the steps of your lesson before filling in the required supplies. It's all about finding the most suitable approach for your teaching style.

Now, let's break down the components of the Curriculum Map:

Objective

The objective is where you express the goal for the workshop.

As a reminder: It should be clear, concise, and measurable with a yes or no. This is all about clear communication. If you can describe the workshop clearly in one sentence, you can communicate your goal (which is also their goal!) to your students. See more details about creating an objective in the *Clarity is Essential: Write an Objective* section.

Methodology

This section involves figuring out the steps you'll teach in your course.

Always begin with background information that will capture your students' interest and is relevant to the craft they're about to dive into.

Let them know who they are trusting their time with by giving them some insight into your personality or telling a fun short story that is relevant to the subject. Share your background and your experience with the subject you're teaching. When they know more about who you are, they will feel more comfortable in your workshop.

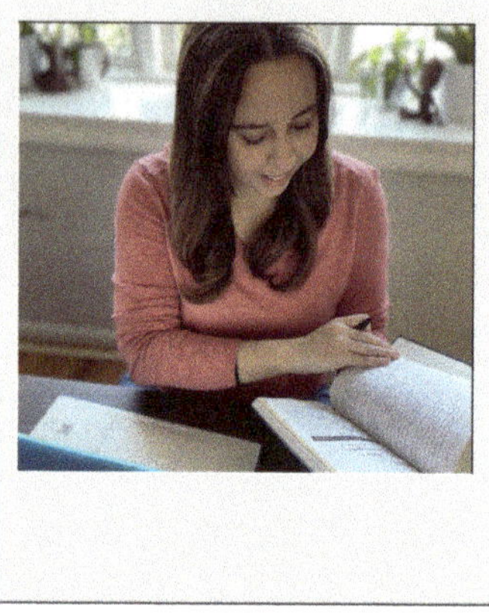

I love to share how I was introduced to quilts. I was nine years old when I made my first quilt, so when I started teaching quilting I had already been quilting for nineteen years! I always got a reaction when I introduced myself by letting them know how much time I had spent in this craft despite being only twenty-eight years old. Then I would go into a story about when I started with the technique (especially if I struggled) or how I started designing patterns if I was teaching a pattern class.

You can keep this short, but it will help them get to know your expertise, build trust with your students, and establish authority. They will then feel like they have made a good and safe investment for their time and money and be ready to learn!

Some other context you can share includes history, stories, and unique vocabulary related to the craft or technique, including your own experiences, as people enjoy engaging with personal stories.

A huge hurdle in entering a craft or learning a new technique is vocabulary. I've entered many workshops, courses, and even corporate training where the instructor speaks in acronyms or terms they use all the time and they completely lose their learners. Take a few seconds to introduce new terms, tools, and supplies that are unique to your craft or technique for any workshop that involves crafters in the beginning to intermediate stages.

Start by building your introduction script:

1. Your name, business name, and what you do for your students.

   Hello! My name is Tori, from The Quilt Patch by Tori. I'm a national teacher, speaker, and quilt pattern designer.

2. Social proof, such as years of experience, number of projects completed or classes taught, or a short factual phrase that can set your authority up front, such as:

   I have been quilting since I was nine years old—I can't believe it's been over twenty years!

3. What are we doing today? This can be stated or you can introduce the topic and objective with a story.

   Today, we will be creating a pillowcase! Why a pillowcase? When I began teaching quilting, I noticed that when it came to completing hefty projects, like a quilt, so many of my beginner students were afraid to cut their fabric and sew on their sewing machine. To learn the basics, we're starting with a small project to [here's the objective!] *learn how to cut efficiently using the rotary cutting tools, learn how to sew a straight ¼-inch seam, and get a good handle on pressing, not ironing. These are all the basic skills you'll need to create a patchwork quilt top! Plus, you'll have a new pillowcase at the end of our class today.*

4. Background information

   We will be using a lot of new terms today. I have a reference sheet for you here. So, when I say… Now, let's get started!

As a reminder, your introduction should only be about 5–7 minutes long. If the technique or pattern you're teaching has a deep, rich history or cultural significance, it may be a little longer but do not exceed fifteen minutes before you have your students start to get hands-on with your workshop. You can always share more history or stories later on in the workshop if you'd like to give more specific information.

Next, you will be diving into the content of your workshop.

Brainstorm and Action Mapping!

Using paper or Post-its, write down each step of the skill or technique. Group the topics and arrange the steps logically from start to finish or basic to advanced.

Identify the foundational steps and progress in a logical sequence. Step 1, Step 2, Step 3, etc., building on itself.

Another way to approach your methodology is to Action Map. The phrase "Action Mapping" was coined by Cathy Moore in Map-it, The Hands-on Guide to Strategic Training Design. The Action Map starts with the objective and then answers the following questions:

- What do you do to achieve this objective?
- If we watch someone (you) do this project, how can we tell whether they understand [topic]? What do they do or *not* do?
- If Tori understands [Topic], but Ryan doesn't, what do they do differently?

Note your answers and the actions you take. You can then organize the notes into actions and subactions. Those actions become your steps, those subactions become your teaching points.

For example:

Action: Bind the finished quilt.

Subactions:

- Sew ¼-inch from the edge leaving a 12-inch tail.
- When I arrive at the corner, I do XYZ...
- To join the edges of the binding using the 12-inch tail, I...
- I finish binding by hand stitching (or machine sewing...).

You now have your steps!

Following the steps of this exercise will help you develop a well-thought-out workshop with a logical flow that feels easy for both you and your students. Having a detailed method can help you anticipate any questions, struggles, or challenges your students will face. It also has the added benefit of helping you plan timing, materials, and what you can prepare in advance to help the workshop flow smoothly (such as prerecorded videos or step-outs). You'll be set up for success and can begin your workshop prepared and confident.

Side Note

I find it helps to take pictures of each little step or record myself running through the process or steps. This helps me keep track of those little steps I've learned with experience that may not be obvious to us, but a game changer to others. You can also use the images for a worksheet or pattern, or to help generate interest in the upcoming workshop!

I do, We do, You do

Now that you have your steps, how are you going to teach these steps?

When introducing a new tool, concept, skill, or technique, *I do, We do, You do* is an excellent tool in your toolbox. This method is based on the Gradual Release of Responsibility Framework. As the instructor, you are responsible for passing on knowledge and you gradually release it to your students, so they can then do that step independently.

It's as literal as it sounds.

First, you as the instructor will demonstrate how you do the step, thinking out loud as you work through that step.

Next, make it collaborative and do it again, this time with the class while you help support them.

Lastly, they will do the step by themselves—independently without you.

In a quilting workshop, this can look like demonstrating free motion quilting designs on your machine first, then having the students try the design with your guidance on their practice quilt sandwich, and finally giving them time to work on the design without help from you.

As a pattern workshop, this can look like having step-outs prepared to show how the technique starts and progresses. You can either walk through the steps showing how the pattern builds or build it with them. Their independent work may be on their own time depending on how long it takes to create the pattern.

You do not have to do this with every step. Take note of your student's skill levels and adjust according to what your students need.

Step-outs

Step-outs are still examples of a project in progress.

Imagine step-outs like a step-by-step picture except they are live examples. For a pattern workshop, these can be a block in the works where the first step-out shows the result of the first two steps of instruction, then the next step-out shows the result of the next two steps, and so on until the block (or quilt) is complete.

For a technique class, they could illustrate the actions mapped in the curriculum map or subactions for a particularly dynamic action step. In other words, you can choose to have step-outs for an entire project or only use them to illustrate different options or more complicated parts of your process. For example, when I taught appliqué, I had step-outs of the same pattern that showed how the finished block would look if they chose to do raw-edge appliqué versus turned-edge appliqué. I have used them to show how different free-motion quilting designs build on themselves and the overall look they create on a quilt square. I have seen other instructors use them to demonstrate different colorways.

I have also used step-outs to illustrate how a quilt is put together for my Learn to Quilt Level 2: The Four Patch Workshop, where they piece together squares to make their first quilt top. This is how I used the step-outs:

Step-out 1: showed the two strips sewed together

Step-outs 2 and 3 respectfully: showed the strip cut and how the four patch blocks were pieced together

Step-out 4: showed how the row looked when those blocks were pieced together

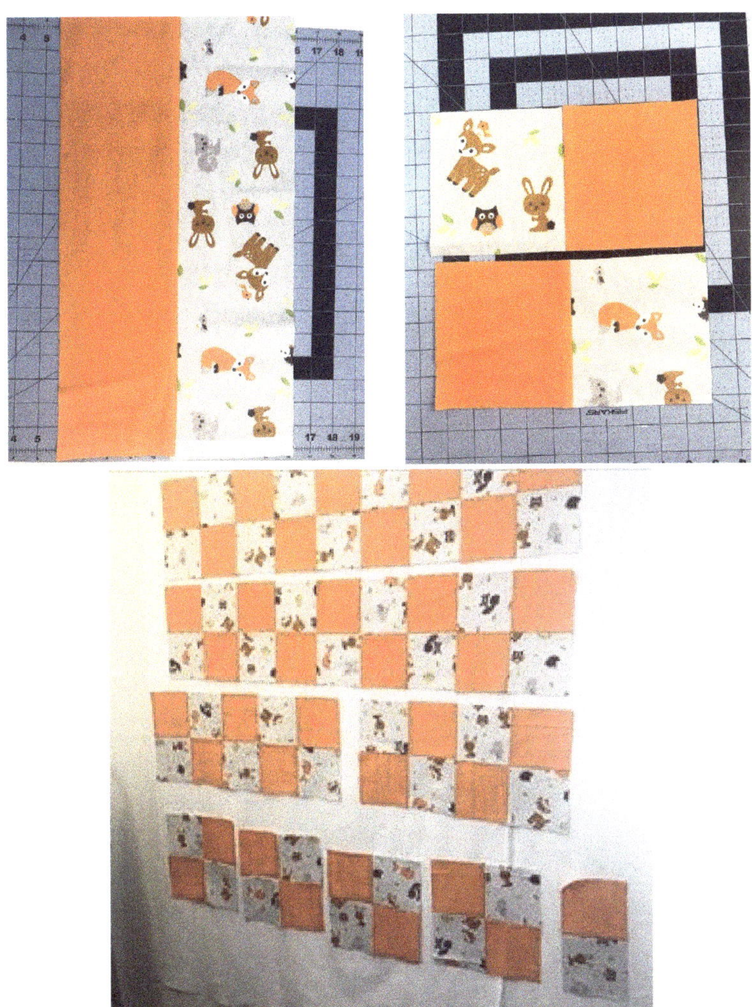

In the pictures above you'll notice these pieces are designed to stick to a design wall. These step-outs were used at my local shop where they had a flannel design wall (much like my personal one pictured here) that I could use to display these step-outs.

Many quilters will display step-outs on small design boards with batting or flannel facing so that the fabric examples can stick and be easily removed. Others will appliqué or fuse the blocks onto a solid-colored fabric (typically white or black, but you can use any color) or muslin for easy storage and display. It depends on how you want to store your step-outs, how often you want to use them, and if you would like the back to be available for the demonstration.

Depending on what you're teaching, steps-out can eliminate the need for you to create the project live for your students, especially if you choose to prerecord yourself and display the videos with the step-outs during the workshop. This works very well if you have availability of technology because it allows you to focus on your students and it will enable them to see your best work. Plus, recording particular steps can also be turned into reference material after the completion of your workshop for your students.

Timing

The next step is to determine how much time each step will take. This is crucial for in-person workshops and live online workshops. You will have limited time with your students and you need to make sure you can achieve your goal within that time frame.

For recorded workshops that students can access at any time, this is slightly less important. You want to try to fit each step in the process under a twenty-minute time frame. However, this is not a hard and fast rule; it's suggested. If you have a few recorded videos that go over twenty minutes, but address the step in its entirety, then let it be as long as it needs to be. If you have steps that take 1–2 minutes, can you group that step with another?

If this is a multi-day, in-person, or live workshop, group your steps based on your time limit for each day. Keep all steps within the time allotted and avoid homework—you don't want them to feel like they're in grade school. There will be instances where they will need to complete a project at home. When teaching a quilt pattern workshop, for example, you will have 2–3 hours to teach the blocks, but the students will need to assemble the top on their own. Your goal in this instance is to be sure they can piece together every type of block in the pattern before they leave your workshop. If it's a simple pattern and you can complete all the blocks before they leave, that's even better. However, if your students don't feel as if they made significant progress, you will have unsatisfied students.

Side Note

If you have requests for a particular pattern or technique that is a time sucker, stand firm on your timing. If you know that no student will be able to get all the information they need in a two-hour workshop, do not commit to a two-hour workshop. I've seen so many quilting and crafting instructors who try to complete a workshop in a shortened time period and it causes frustration on all 3 sides: the students, the instructors, and the host.

In the grand scheme of things, keep your workshop moving or changing every 10–20 minutes. I keep this time a little loose because it depends on how they are doing and what you are teaching. There's nothing worse for me than when I have students fall asleep in a workshop. Now, this has never happened in the public workshops, however, as a tech trainer, it tends to happen with every training class because there's very little opportunity to change up what we are doing.

This change or movement can be as simple as having them turn and talk, move to another section of the room, or if this workshop is virtual, changing camera angles. Let them get hands-on with the information as soon as possible.

With the class example above where I used to teach quilting basics, I would run through my introduction, have them introduce themselves and how long they've been quilting (usually not long), and then we would all move together to the cutting table where I would demonstrate how to use the rotary tools. Then, it would be their turn. I had three stations set up around the workshop space so they could pick a spot and get to cutting.

You can see that in twenty minutes my students have been through four changes and three separate physical areas. This movement and change keep them energized, focused, and engaged!

One question that pops up around time management is the timing for a multiple-day workshop where students come together (virtually or in person) for a few hours and then go home and meet again at a later date to complete or make progress on the project. Consider how much time they need to complete the steps you've gone over in the workshop and whether they will need time to complete part of the workshop at home. I do dissuade homework, however, with some crafts and quilting projects, you may not be able to avoid it.

If it's your first time hosting this particular kind of workshop or topic, look at what other instructors have done. Are they having their students meet weekly? Bi-weekly? Every other day? Choose what you think may be best from this research and your experience, and use your student's feedback to adjust. Also, don't be afraid to add in an "implementation day" or "down week" to give them time on a particularly lengthy project. In my Master Color Class that I hosted for ten weeks, I incorporated two weeks of "make-up days" where students who had missed a live class could request a topic to go over (these color classes could only be hosted live as per my certification contract, but I made it work!). Be sure to see what other instructors have done and adjust your time in the future based on the feedback you get from your students.

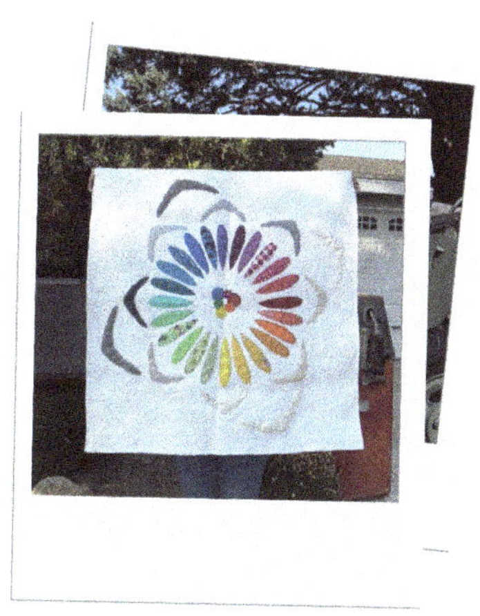

Demonstrating Mastery: It's Not What You Think!

Understanding what mastery means for your workshop is crucial. It's not about students perfecting a skill or pattern in a single class, rather, it's about achieving the workshop objective. Determine how your students will *demonstrate* mastery and make sure they understand how they can assess their progress. This clarity is essential to ensure your students leave the class feeling successful and fulfilled.

For example, mastery in a quilting workshop could mean completing a specific block for a pattern that they can then complete on their own. It could be practicing various quilting motifs on a practice panel to show their progress on free motion quilting. Will they be able to create perfect loops and swirls with the stitching on their quilt tops after a single class? Maybe, but most likely they will need practice. Having the practice panel as a physical example of their skills is a powerful representation of progress and learning.

You want them to be able to see without a doubt that they can now do the skill or technique they set out to learn. They need to have a physical example to prove to themselves that they are successful and can build up their skill or finish the pattern on their own.

When students feel successful, they come back to learn more and they usually tell or bring a friend!

Do not skip demonstrating mastery, do not pass go and collect $200 (or host this workshop you're planning) without a plan for your students to demonstrate that they have had a successful workshop.

Reaching All Learners

Learning styles are a myth; humans don't learn in one way. Instead, we use our whole brain to learn. I have studied about how humans learn in several different ways over a decade of formal education and teaching, and I'd like to share an efficient way to address whole-brain learning. You can activate whole-brain learning by appealing to different senses and by using different types of social support in your workshop. While you don't have to provide experiences for every sense or every social structure, the more senses you try to support, the better the learning and the more satisfied your students will be.

The idea here is to get you thinking of the different ways you can support your students. The list below is for idea generation.

Visual Learning Support:

You can support your learners with pictures, diagrams, charts, maps, videos, and other visual aids to demonstrate what you're teaching and for their future reference. One of the best strategies I've heard and used is giving your students access to a recorded version of the workshop. Depending on the workshop, it can be at a discount or free for a limited time. This strategy can be used for digital and in-person workshops. Imagine the value they will receive when they realize they can reference the instruction at any time as they work on the skill, pattern, or technique on their own!

Auditory Learning Support:

Speak to your students in a clear, appropriately loud volume, but also one-on-one. Have them discuss and speak out loud to either you or each other during the workshop to reiterate what they're learning. This also includes videos for support after the workshop or even access to audio recordings like a podcast so they can listen on the go.

Kinesthetic Learning Support:

We usually have this one in the bag! A workshop is typically hands-on learning. We are creating or putting the technique, skill, or even theory to work with materials that our students can touch, move, and feel. If your workshop does not have activities that include using their hands, is there a way you can incorporate them?

Color theory is a great example that many quilters and crafters study. You can just teach the theory, but the lesson is more powerful when your students get to work with the materials they will be using when they apply color theory. If you're a quilting instructor, break out that fabric and get your students experimenting with the material.

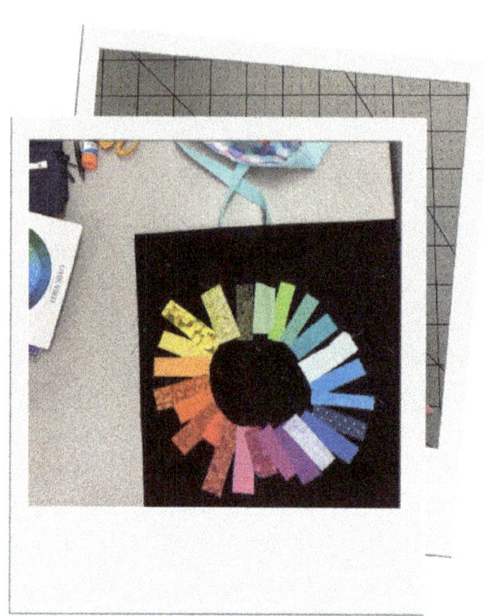

Reading and Writing Learning Support:

Having the steps written out clearly is just as important as providing clear images for your learners. Pattern designers rely heavily on the process of taking their actions and putting them into words and phrases that can translate well to anyone in their craft. Be sure you have your steps described clearly. You can ask a novice to read over your written process to make sure it is clear to them. Reference your favorite written patterns to see what terms they've used for different steps. However, be mindful of copyright law. Do not copy and paste their steps without expressed permission.

You can also use AI to help you clear up any confusing sentences, adjust tone, check spelling and grammar, and outline a worksheet.

Logical Learning Support:

Logical learners love, love, love, clear steps that build on each other. After that awesome (if I do say so myself) Methodology section, I'm sure your actions are laid out very logically. Take it one step further and clearly define these steps for your students during and after the workshop with your supporting materials.

Social Learning Support:

Let them socialize. Make some time for it. They are here to learn, have fun, and socialize. Socializing is also a great way to commit what they are learning to memory. They will share ideas, complement each other, joke, celebrate, reiterate what may have been confusing (helping you know where to improve!), and share a fun experience inside a space that you have created. They will feel like their time is well spent and they will want to come back for more!

Solitary Learning Support:

Many quilters and crafters are more successful when they learn alone. I learn complicated techniques better alone and not in an actual workshop environment. Having materials they can take with them is an amazing way to support their learning. You will also find that many who learn better on their own will also reach out days or weeks after the workshop to ask questions. Having supporting materials ready to reference, will make your role as the instructor a lot easier. Some ideas have been discussed above, and you can find a list in the Supplemental Materials section of this book.

You can support many of these with your supporting materials, check out the next section!

Last Note About Support:

You will have students who will be challenged in many ways. You do *not* have to do everything listed above, but the more senses you can appeal to and the more teaching styles that you can incorporate, the more successful your students will feel. If your students feel successful, they will come back to learn more. They may even bring a friend.

Also, consider some overall advice to help students overcome challenges to learning:

- have a well-lit room or workspace on camera
- provide a larger font (12–16pt font) on your worksheets or patterns
- colored images that show details
- project your voice, speaking clearly
- project images on a screen so everyone can see the detail in your demonstrations

These are not only great teaching practices, but they can assist those with an array of challenges.

Terminology

Vocabulary, technical terms, and niche-specific terms are the largest barriers for new crafters. Clarifying terms while working through your project in a workshop, defining these terms as you introduce them, and making sure you are defining any acronyms, will bridge that gap for a new crafter. If you're teaching beginners, consider providing a terminology sheet that can help support the newest crafters in your workshop.

Tools

What tools do they need and how do they use them?

These can be physical tools, a workbook, or a reference. Taking a few moments to go over the names and use of the tools that your students will be using in the workshop is a great way to support your new crafters.

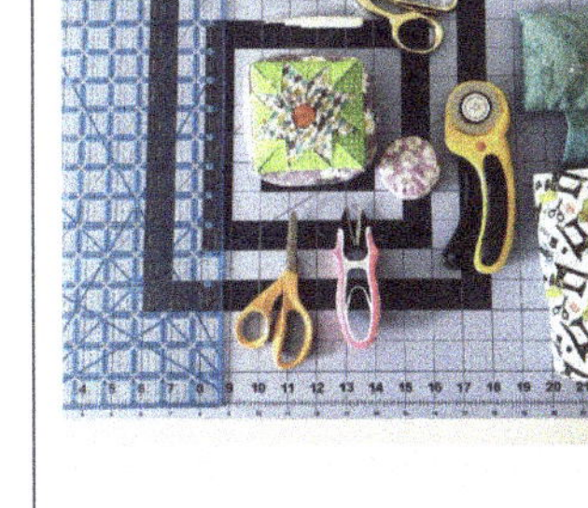

Just to clarify, if you have experienced crafters in your workshop, you will not need to go over every tool. However, sharing your favorite ones and any new tools will help set up your workshop for success!

Also, I would caution you about assumptions. Many experienced crafters appreciate the reminder or if they are self-taught, appreciate the overview of tools most frequently used to get to know more craft-specific terminology. It also helps your more experienced learners feel prepared as you go over which tools the workshop will be using.

For example, if quilters are signing up for a longarm quilting workshop to learn a more moderate to advanced technique, you can safely assume that they have quilted on a longarm. However, sharing your favorite thread, scissors, needles, or other notions (tools) you prefer to use for this technique *and how or why you use them* can add immense value and support for your learners.

Materials

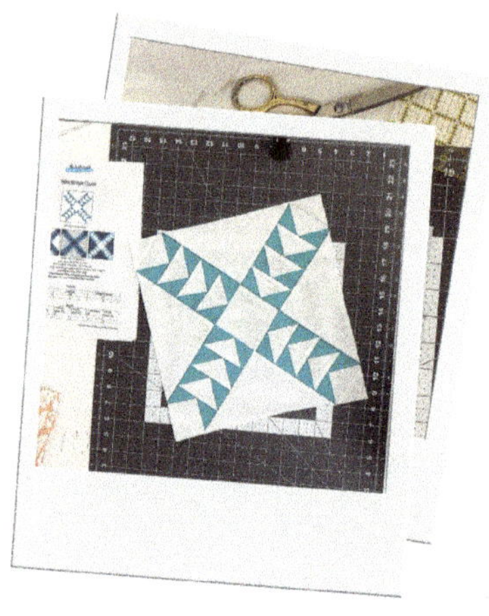

Having a list of materials is essential for both you as the instructor and your students.

You'll want to document a materials list for yourself and a separate one for your students.

As a quilting or crafting teacher, you may be booked a month or a year in advance. You may be hired to teach a workshop next week and then four months or even a year later be hired to teach it again. Having a list of materials for yourself and your students can save you a ton of time and energy when preparing your workshop after a long time away.

As for a materials list for your students, be sure you've written a detailed list. If you're using thread, what kind of thread? What color? What kind of needle? Do they need to print anything ahead of time? What will you as the instructor be providing? Be as specific as you can. A detailed materials list can help your students feel prepared and show up ready to learn.

If this is a workshop held online, do they need a large device? Many crafting workshops are better if they have a larger screen to see the details—a phone would not be ideal. However, if it is more discussion-based, a phone can be just fine.

The more detailed, the better. Your students will feel well-prepared for their workshop and will already experience a high level of support that will demonstrate your authority and establish some trust before they even get there!

Supplemental Materials

Supplemental materials are essential for ensuring your students' success even after the workshop is over. They act as valuable resources for further learning and practice. Consider including 1–5 of the supports listed below. Some examples may be beneficial for digital workshops while others are more suited for in person workshops. You can decide what fits your workshop.

- A pattern(s)
- An exclusive pattern(s)
- Articles about the specific skill
- Tip sheet(s)
- A checklist
- A planner
- Templates
- Workbooks that they can fill in
- Practice sheet(s)
- A specialized or useful tool
- A gook or guide (physical or an ebook)
- Free or discounted prerecorded version of the workshop
- A free or discounted prerecorded version of the next stage of the skill/technique they learned
- Short video tutorials on specific steps or processes

- Interview series for examples, stories, or inspiration
- Blogs/virtual articles tailored to the content of the class
- Audio files (like a specialized podcast)
- An accountability group
- Follow-up with an event, retreat, or other social gathering
- Offer office hours or consultations

These supplemental materials have the added benefit of enhancing the value of your class. They reinforce learning and can greatly enhance the success of your students after the workshop ends. However, you want to be picky when choosing which ones to add to your workshop. You don't want to give them more to do if it's not going to help them master the skill, technique, or pattern. Your focus should be on how to ensure your students master what they learn efficiently (easily and quickly) and what you can offer to support that.

Narrowing Down What You Need

If you're having trouble narrowing down exactly what needs to be included in your workshop materials, steps, and the project itself, think back to the objective and consider your overall purpose of the workshop. In the book, *The Art of the Gathering,* Priya Parker writes about digging deeper to find your purpose of a gathering, and from there you'll be able to pinpoint what you need to include.

In our case, the gathering is a workshop. However, let's take this purpose and dig a little deeper to pull out any underlying purposes of why we are gathering for a workshop.

Take your initial purpose and ask yourself "why" *at least* three times to really get to the heart of why you're having people gather for a workshop.

The first why could look like this: Why are we gathering to learn about free motion quilting? *They want to learn a new skill in their quilting craft in person.*

Second why: Why do they want to learn a new skill? *They are looking for a creative outlet, to enhance their skills, and help them feel connected to a community and tradition.*

Third why: Why are they looking for a creative outlet, new skills, and a tie to community and tradition? *Creativity and community are essential parts of the human experience—both create joy (ideally). They want to learn something new, keep their minds sharp, have fun with like-minded people, and be able to make their creative ideas come to life.*

Each question brings more clarity to why we are hosting this particular workshop. If you're grappling with the question of adding discussion time to your workshop, use this purpose to determine if it's a good addition. In our example, community building is part of the purpose, so we would add discussion time. However, if this is a prerecorded workshop, the purpose is purely to learn a new skill, and therefore, the answer would be no, there's no need to include discussion within the lessons.

Let's consider the question of background information. For a beginner free motion quilting workshop, is a history of free motion quilting needed? If the purpose is to continue the tradition of quilting, a quick evolution may be interesting to those attending, however, it may be more beneficial to explain what free motion quilting is in a skill-based workshop.

After all, the purpose of the gathering is to learn how to do the skill, not to learn about the skill's history.

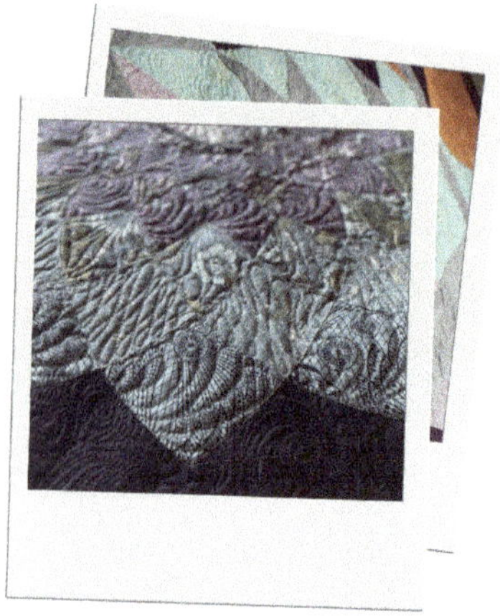

If excluding information makes you hesitate, keep in mind that the ultimate way you can serve your students is to help them solve their problems and learn this new skill, technique, or pattern efficiently and effectively. If including history disrupts the effectiveness or efficiency of a workshop, then it can be excluded.

By carefully considering these components, you'll be well on your way to designing a fantastic and engaging course that leaves a lasting impact on your students.

Take Action and Teach!

It's time to take action. It seems simple, but turning the plan into action is a hill many instructors start climbing, only to roll back down and never actually teach their beautifully designed workshop.

If actually teaching what you've planned feels like an uphill climb, start small. Teach friends first, or if you're a part of a guild or crafting group, start there. If that still feels like a mountain, invite one person to teach. It can be as informal as asking them to help you walk through your workshop. That's the only way you will be able to catch any actions or subactions you may have missed. It's the only way to see what others will have questions about and what unexpected challenges they may face. Then teach a group and get more feedback.

The best way to get better at teaching is to teach. This book can be a guide to help you prepare and give you ideas on how to level up your instruction, but nothing can replace experience.

"Confidence is the successful repetition of any endeavor" - Debbie Millman

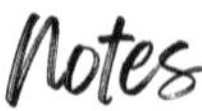

"You miss 100% of the shots you don't take"
- **Wayne Gretzky**

What's Better—a Live or Recorded Workshop?

This question can stop any quilting or crafting instructor in their tracks! Are you jumping back and forth and not making any progress? You're not alone.

This is one of the top questions I get asked by my students and clients. Should they pre-record and sell their workshop as a digital product, host the workshop live, or only teach their workshop in person?

The answer is…

It depends! You may have seen that coming, but it's true!

There are pros and cons for both, but the real answer lies in the purpose of why you're even creating a workshop. The purpose lies in the "why" that's deeper than the objective or goal of the workshop.

Recall the activity from the book *The Art of Gathering*. Priya Parker asks her clients "why" until they get to the true purpose of the gathering they want to host.

In our case, we're looking at a workshop. I would invite you to go at least three "whys" deep—deeper if you need to. Ask yourself, "Why do I want to host a workshop?"

"*I want to answer all these frequently asked questions that all students ask me*"

Why?

"*To take work off my plate, but still keep the students wanting to learn more with me*"

Why?

"*I want to grow my main workshop attendance and move them from the FAQs to my main workshop where I can teach them my unique technique (or pattern!)*"

Ah-Ha!

If your purpose is to move them quickly to the next step, your unique technique or pattern, *then* you need to decide whether you need to host this live or recorded.

Pros to hosting live or in person:

- Build connection with your students
- Build community
- Can be more discussion-based and bounce ideas off each other
- Answer all their questions, provide unique examples, and tweak your content based on who is present
- Spend less time in front of a camera
- Can cost more or less depending on where you're hosting
- Can be a great revenue stream, if you've chosen to charge for it

Cons to hosting live or in person:

- You have to block off time
- Choosing a time. Some clients are in different time zones or have busy/full schedules
- Cost (depending on where you're hosting)
- A lot of work for you to set up each time you host
- A lot of energy with each workshop

Pros of creating a recorded workshop:

- The brunt of the work is upfront
- Students can take it at any time, or you can open/close it at any time
- You can send clients back to the workshop if they need to review information
- Can be a stream of revenue with little work

Cons to creating a recorded workshop:

- No discussion opportunities
- You can't provide a unique experience or examples for those present in the workshop
- Less connection and trust development (there's still some, but significantly less)
- Learning about different platforms and choosing where to host
- You have to keep it updated
- Editing—it can take twice as long to edit a workshop as it does to record it
- Perfectionism tends to get in the way of so many when they're creating a recorded workshop

There may be more to add and consider for yourself, but from the list above, what sounds like it will fit your purpose?

Our example's purpose was to move your students quickly through the FAQs to your main workshop where you want to teach them your unique techniques or pattern. This sounds like a recorded workshop. However, if you had dived deeper and decided to use this workshop as an opportunity to build your community that is spread around the world, a live workshop where discussion and connection can happen may be the best way to follow your purpose. However, if you have physical limitations or time constraints, a hybrid of a recorded workshop and live Q&A or social meetings could support the purpose of building community.

Dive into what your true purpose is for the workshop. Truly consider what this workshop is for, and it will light the way to your format of recorded or live.

Price to Thrive

When I started teaching quilting workshops I was inspired to launch a block-of-the-month program. I was about seven months into business and had a successful beginner series I taught live online and in person at my local quilt shop. These beginner quilters were so excited to jump into all the quilting skills that I rose to the challenge with an idea I had percolating in the back of my mind.

I designed and set up a year-long, block-of-the-month program teaching four different piecing skills—one skill for each quarter of the year, which I called the Skill Building Block of the Month. It took months to prepare! I taught myself turned edge appliqué (I knew raw edge when I started, but not turned edge appliqué), I learned quilt pattern design software, mocked up and wrote twelve patterns and a sample for each pattern, plus a few design options based on which skills they focused on. I taught each block live, recorded it, edited it, and inserted it into a recorded program with supporting materials. The members had their own Facebook Group and unlimited access to me for questions. It was a ton of time, energy, and resources. I only charged $12 a month. Ugh. If I could go back and redo it, I would have doubled the price, maybe even tripled it, because I had also added how to finish the quilt! It was all too much.

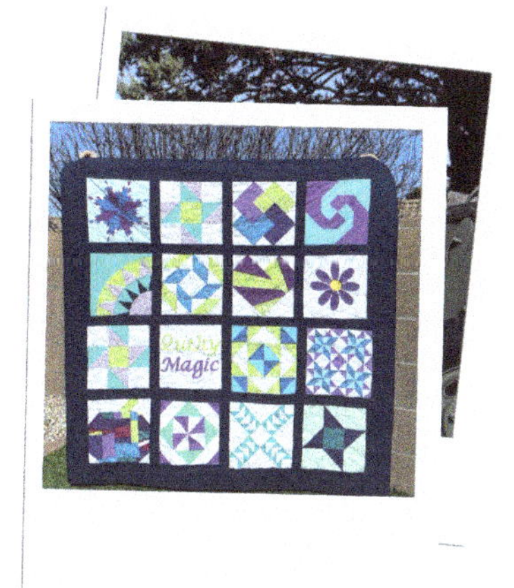

I had not created conditions for myself to thrive. I was running on fumes keeping it all up to date and staying in contact with the members while also trying to keep my business afloat. Therefore, I also had not created conditions for the program and for my students to thrive. If I had charged double, I would have had fewer members (or maybe not) and more revenue. And since I had a toddler at the time, that extra revenue could have provided more daycare for more time and energy to support this wonderful program and my students.

I'm imploring you to price to thrive—for your sake and your students' sake.

Pricing needs to create conditions for you to thrive as a teacher and a business. Regardless of whether you're teaching on the side or creating a full-time business with your workshops, you need to be sure that what you are charging is allowing you to supply the necessary time, energy, and literal supplies for this workshop. Consider what conditions you need to provide for yourself and your students and make sure your price reflects that.

When we price to thrive, we are charging for value and not for time. Consider how this workshop will impact your students' lives. How much money, time, and resources will they save by being a part of this workshop? What will they be able to accomplish after your workshop? You're charging for the solution and transformation you're offering in this workshop, not how much time it takes for you to prepare the materials and teach it.

In 2018, when I decided to start sewing and selling baby quilts, I knew it was time to learn how to free-motion quilt. At the time, I had a small Singer sewing machine with a 6-inch throat—a very small space to squeeze a quilt into! I couldn't find a class near me and YouTube had become popular for learning new skills, so I watched video after video of quilters free motion quilting. I read blogs about tips for free motion quilting. I went to my local JoAnns (there were no local quilt stores where I was at the time) and ordered the right foot for my machine. I bought some scrap fabric and spent hours breaking needles and ruining the tension on my machine trying to quilt with "quilting thread."

I broke down and called my mom. My mom is an award-winning free-motion longarm quilter. She quilts free hand on a 12-foot table, stitching beautiful designs onto quilts for herself and her clients...and I wasted weeks trying to teach myself. She quickly informed me I had the wrong thread (turns out that thread was for hand quilting!) and gave me some valuable advice.

What I wouldn't have paid to just take a class! A simple Free-Motion Quilting 101 class! It would have saved me so much time, energy, money, materials, and stress! I was so motivated to learn and had no teacher. It would have been well worth the $65 I charged for my Intro to Free Motion Quilting Workshop I started teaching two years later.

Another factor to consider is how your pricing will look to your future students. Your price will determine how they treat you and what you're teaching. Undercharging will attract students who make purchasing options based on price rather than on value. Underpricing your workshop tends to bring students who don't commit, are not fully participatory, and tend to be very demanding and not enthusiastic about what they're learning. You will still find a few of these Grumpy Gus's in your workshop, but by charging by value you'll find less and less of them as you draw in your ideal student. You'll also have more energy to help your Grumpy Gus's thrive in your workshop.

If you haven't been convinced that you may be undercharging yet, please consider other teachers in the craft industry. Undercharging hurts the industry and your collaborators (notice I did not say competitors—we are all in this together).

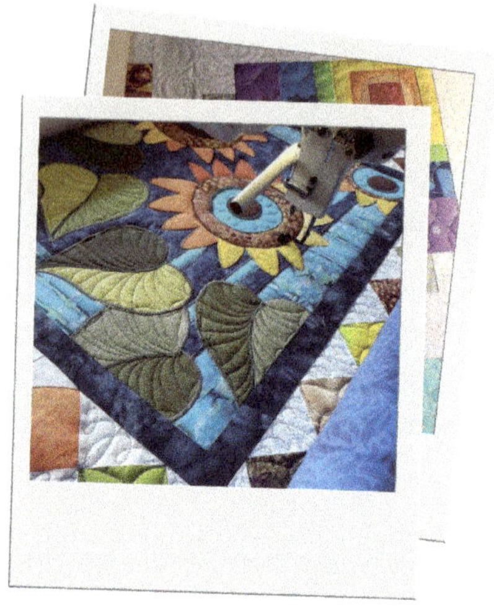

The craft industry is growing. It is predicted to grow to a $50.9 billion industry in 2024 worldwide (ScottMax Citation). According to the study done by Needle Arts in 2023, the quilting industry specifically is predicted to almost double. They predicted that "the strength of the Quilt Market will continue to provide solid growth, approaching $5 billion by 2026–2027." That same report also describes the state of the overall sewist community. In 2023, there were "over 85 million 'active creatives' in the U.S. and Canada, representing more than $35 billion in sales (defined as individuals who have made a creative project in the past 12 months)."

There is an "estimated 30 million active sewists, which has had a slight decrease since the pandemic years. The "quilt industry continues to have steady annual growth rates at GDP+ with 9 million to 11 million active quilters, which has remained consistent over the last 10 years." Wow!

These statistics show that there is room for you to thrive in the crafting space. With millions of potential students who are looking to create using their sewing machines!

Another factor to take into account is money and what women can do with it. Currently, the craft industry is a female-led market. Making money should not be a bad thing. Money itself is neutral—a tool to be used. Nothing bad happens when women make more money. Studies show that women who make extra revenue are more likely to invest in their families, local communities, and charities. Imagine what you could do with extra revenue for yourself, your family, and even your local community.

Pick a Number

Let's get down to pricing strategy and actually pick a number.

First, get to know what your ideal student is already paying for a similar workshop. Do a little research and ask around. Many craft groups have professional teachers who are fully happy to share their pricing structure. Many more have their pricing listed online.

Get obsessed with testimonials and feedback. You can use this information to get to know your ideal student and be able to create workshops that service them best. Testimonials also provide a second voice for your business and help show how other people have had wonderful experiences in your workshops (more in the feedback section).

Do the math on your value. Consider the following questions:

- How much have you spent learning the skill and designing the pattern or technique you now want to teach?
- How much time have you spent learning?
- How much training or any type of education have you had (self-taught counts)?
- How much experience in years do you have?

- Does the math add up? Does your pricing reflect your value?

Recall the Skill Building Block of the Month example that I spent roughly two years fully developing. I had eighteen years of quilting experience when I began that process, three years of teaching public education, and a Masters degree in Education. I spent countless hours that first year in business learning different types of technology and even a few piecing techniques I wasn't familiar with as well as providing one-on-one attention with 24/7 availability (because I had poor boundaries). All of a sudden that $12 a month doesn't add up to the value I was providing.

Make your workshop irresistible to your ideal student by creating an experience where you provide a better or faster result. This may require you to take things out of your workshop to achieve this goal fully. In the Skill Building Block of the Month, I fully regret adding in extra instruction on finishing a quilt. I felt pressured by the idea that a few of my beginner quilters had followed me from Learn to Quilt Level 1 through all four skills and wanted to be told how to finish the quilt (even though I had provided those basics in the beginner series). I truly believe that adding in that instruction was unneeded for my ideal student who already knew those basics and wouldn't want to pay for the knowledge they already had. In addition, I could have had even better results had I just stuck with the skills as separate workshops, which I eventually did for in-person workshops at my local quilt shop. Being able to teach exactly what your ideal student is looking for is highly valuable.

For highly-priced courses or memberships, consider payment tiers or specific tracks your students could choose, and allow them to choose the price that fits their budget. These can look like:

- Offering a monthly cost or a yearly cost for access to a course.
- Bundling your courses with a community where they have more access to you or offering just the instruction at a lower price.
- Offering workshops for each pattern as an upsell to that pattern or offering membership access to all patterns and all workshops.

Price to thrive and expect your students to pay your price. You do not have to justify to them what your value is. You can demonstrate it with your description (see the Objective section for more), provide testimonials, and show them what's included. But when it's time to state your price, say it with confidence.

Rachel Rodgers, who wrote *We Should All Be Millionaires* and who inspired me to include this section, wrote, "When you double your prices, everyone wins...You win. Your clients win. Your family wins. Your community wins." So when in doubt, double your price. Compare it to your pricing research, do the math, and make sure the value adds up. Then deliver that price with confidence.

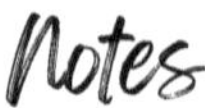

"We are allowed to be ambitious for ambition's sake - unapologetically."

-Rachel Rodgers

Meet Your Students

Walking into a workshop you'll never know what kind of personalities you will encounter. You will have a wonderful mix of strangers, close friends, acquaintances, and possibly a sprinkle of contentious history.

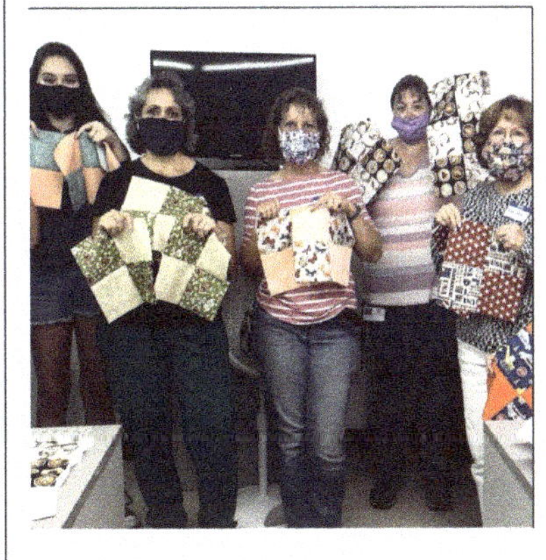

One of my most memorable classes had a mix of four very different personalities, but we were all there to share our love of quilting. There was an eighteen-year-old college student who did everything by the book and sat slightly apart from everyone. There was a dressmaker of fifty-plus years who was anxious to learn perfect piecing; a quilter of about twelve years who was a wealth of knowledge and came just to learn the pillowcase project; and a brand new quilter who had just unpacked her machine and instantly became BFFs with everyone around her.

We had a great time gently urging the youngest to share her excellent fabric pull, patiently answering all of the questions from the newest quilter, hearing the experience of the most experienced quilter in the workshop, and cheering on the seasoned dressmaker who used the rotary cutter for the first time. In those two hours, everyone created a functional pillowcase and left the class with new friends!

To help these different personalities succeed in your workshop, they will need a few different things: a caring approach, a little strategy, and a dash of action. Let's meet your students.

The Expert: Expert Edna

She is a wealth of knowledge and loves to share! She's a learner at heart and is there for the fun of learning all the hows, whys, and why-nots. She has been creating in your craft for years, possibly decades and she will have great tips that she can share.

- Approach: Engage them by asking about their experience and expertise.

- Strategy: Encourage them to share their knowledge and advice with the class.

- Action: Showcase their work and express gratitude for their contributions, fostering a sense of validation and camaraderie.

The A-Plus Student: Studious Stacey

She likes to do things by the book. Studious Stacy will love the handouts, worksheets, and/or step-by-step directions in your workshop. If you don't have any supporting materials, be prepared for a little frustration from Studious Stacey and encourage them to embrace the process.

If you have a studious Stacy in an online workshop, this learner is an amazing participant. They will do everything they can to show up on time to every live call, follow your process to a T, and they are an excellent student to get feedback from.

- Approach: Recognize their commitment to excellence and desire for mastery.

- Strategy: Provide challenging tasks or additional resources to fuel their ambition.

- Action: Offer personalized feedback and encouragement, acknowledging their achievements while encouraging continuous growth.

The Collaborator: Talkative Tina

Talkative Tina is the extrovert in the room. This student can't help but answer all questions, share their opinions, and engage those around them. Talkative Tina needs dedicated time to talk, they are attending a workshop for the community. Let them know when it's appropriate to talk but keep an eye out for side quests—we've got one mission in a workshop, and you don't want a side quest to derail the project.

Talkative Tina is also an excellent leader. If you're planning to break into pairs or small groups, partner a Talkative Tina with a Tenacious Tisha and watch their project blossom.

- Approach: Appreciate their enthusiasm for teamwork and cooperative learning.

- Strategy: Facilitate group projects and collaborative exercises to harness their collaborative spirit.

- Action: Add in discussion time and encourage peer-to-peer feedback, and mutual support, fostering a sense of community and shared accomplishment.

Slow and Steady: Methodical Martha

Methodical Martha is our turtle in this Hare and Turtle race. Slow and steady. This learner will want to dive into every step in their own time and in their own way. They may be similar to a Studious Stacy and follow your directions to a T or they will disregard everything you've laid out for them and proceed to complete the project the way they see fit—it could seriously go either way.

- Approach: Respect their deliberate pace and attention to detail.

- Strategy: Provide ample time and resources for thorough comprehension and practice. Make sure they have what they need to finish the project on their own time. Give strategic breaks to allow them time to catch up.

- Action: Offer one-on-one guidance and patience, emphasizing progress over speed. Make sure they have what they need to finish the project on their own time. Offering to go over a few things before they leave may also go a long way in helping this student succeed.

The Binger: Deep Dive Debbie

Deep Dive Debbie is a student who may seem like a procrastinator, but she prefers to see the whole picture before diving in and completing the whole project. You'll notice Deep Dive Debbies a lot easier in a virtual workshop where they wait until all the content is out before diving in.

Having follow-up check-ins with your virtual students will be very valuable to a Deep Dive Debbie to get her questions answered after they have gone through all the content.

- Approach: Recognize their tendency to immerse themselves fully in the learning process.

- Strategy: Channel their enthusiasm into structured learning experiences.

- Action: Provide varied and engaging activities to sustain their interest while ensuring a balanced approach to learning.

The Planner: Logical Lisa

Logical Lisa likes all the information ahead of time. This student feels most comfortable in a workshop with a schedule, a syllabus (if this workshop is more than a day), and a clear goal. They like to know when the breaks are, the general steps, and the flow of the workshop. Logical Lisa also loves structure within the workshop. Sharing break times and the general plan of the workshop will help Logical Lisa feel more at ease and prepared.

- Approach: Appreciate their organized and methodical approach to learning.

- Strategy: Offer clear objectives and structured lesson plans to align with their preference for structure.

- Action: Provide detailed instructions and resources in advance, allowing them to prepare effectively and maximize their learning experience.

The Wildcard: Daring Darla

Daring Darla is a student who mixes a few of these personalities, and you never really know what they're going to do but they're up for trying anything. In a virtual workshop, Daring Darla will be present about half the time and surprise you with a finished project at the end or four months later.

- Approach: Embrace their unpredictability and willingness to explore new ideas.

- Strategy: Encourage experimentation and creativity while providing guidance and support.

- Action: Foster a flexible and adaptive learning environment that celebrates individuality and innovation.

The Introvert: Tenacious Tisha

This personality is named after my wonderful twin sister, Tisha. She is the very definition of a tenacious introvert. She's there to be creative, loves to observe, wants to learn and try something new, but won't say much at all. Mainly, this student uses their voice to praise or clear up any confusion. Watch their facial expressions for frustrations and encourage participation.

- Approach: Respect their need for solitude and reflection.

- Strategy: Create opportunities for quiet introspection and individualized instruction such as stopping by their workstation and checking in for questions.

- Action: Offer alternative communication channels such as written feedback or small group discussions to accommodate their preferences. Virtually, this could look like email or inviting live participants to type in the chat.

The Perfectionist: Perfect Paula

"Perfectionism is just fear in fancy shoes" – Elizabeth Gilbert in *Big Magic*.

Perfect Paula has reservations about their skill unless it's perfect. They are in your workshop to learn how to do their craft to perfection. Many Perfect Paulas will place emphasis on *the right way* to do something when there may be several ways to accomplish a step or to finish a process. There is a whole science devoted to helping perfectionism, but some quick and easily deployable advice is to create a welcoming environment where they can feel safe to demonstrate their imperfections as they learn.

- Approach: Understand their desire for flawlessness and attention to detail.

- Strategy: Encourage risk-taking and acceptance of imperfection as part of the creative process.

- Action: Emphasize the beauty of uniqueness and personal expression, fostering a supportive environment where mistakes are viewed as learning opportunities. Also, do not force them to share.

The Time-Conscious: Overscheduled Olivia

Overscheduled Olivia is one of the reasons why we try our best to fit everything or at least the essential building blocks of a project, process, or pattern into the time allotted for workshops. Overscheduled Olivia only has so much time to devote to a craft. Ensure that they can finish on time. If this is a virtual workshop, encourage them to follow up when available.

- Approach: Understand their busy schedules and limited availability.

- Strategy: Offer flexible workshop formats such as short sessions or weekend intensives to accommodate their time constraints.

- Action: Provide concise and focused instruction, maximizing learning within limited timeframes while offering opportunities for continued practice and support beyond the workshop.

The Self-Doubter: Humble Holly

Humble Holly may surprise you. This student will downplay their ability or experience and may be over-critical of their project. They may emphasize how great other students' projects are and ignore their own project. I have even seen some Humble Hollys physically hide what they're working on in class.

- Approach: Recognize their insecurities and fear of failure.

- Strategy: Provide encouragement and positive reinforcement to boost their confidence. Emphasize what they are excelling at.

- Action: Offer constructive feedback and celebrate their progress, nurturing a supportive environment where self-doubt is replaced with self-assurance and pride in their accomplishments.

The Innovator: Creative Casey

Creative Casey is a bit of a rare find inside a workshop, but they are a diamond in the rough. I truly enjoy watching a Creative Casey take the process, pattern, or technique that is being taught and use it to create or even improve upon the content or the project.

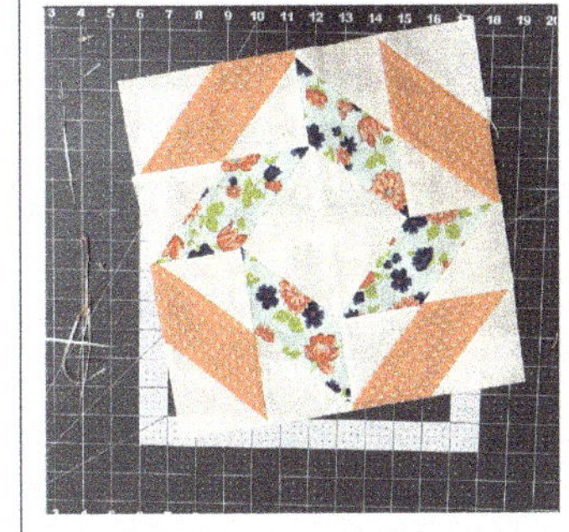

- Approach: Emphasize what should be followed structurally so the project doesn't fall apart but embrace their creativity and forward-thinking mindset.

- Strategy: Encourage experimentation and exploration of unconventional techniques and materials.

- Action: Provide opportunities for brainstorming and idea-sharing, fostering a culture of innovation and creative problem-solving within the workshop community.

Every workshop has a mix of different personalities, and as an instructor, it's important to understand your students to help them succeed. Each student has unique needs, and acknowledging them can help create a supportive and inclusive learning environment. By appreciating their strengths, providing personalized strategies, and fostering a sense of community you can help your students learn and grow together.

If you'd like to see more strategies for supporting your students, there are more suggestions in the Reaching All Learners section. Keep in mind that you do not have to put every one of these strategies and actions in every workshop. Use them as they fit your type of workshop and the personalities you encounter.

Meet Your Colleagues Podcast

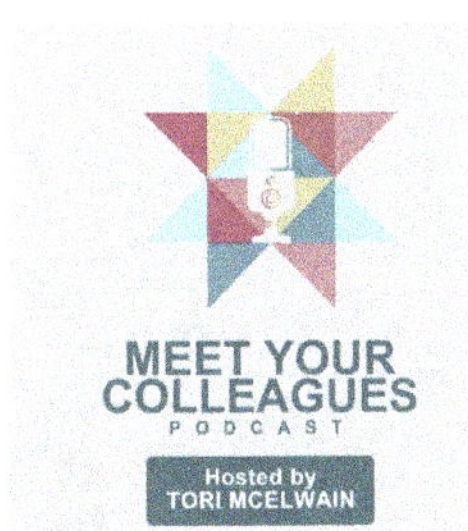

You've met *Your Students*, it's now time to Meet Your Colleagues!

Follow the QR Code below to the secret Meet Your Colleagues Podcast where you will hear interviews with crafting teachers from around the world. They share their personal stories, insights, and best advice for new and established teachers.

Meet Your Colleagues Podcast Link

Step 1: Hold your smartphone camera up to the QR code and tap on the link that pops up.

Or you can take a picture of this page and on your smartphone tap and hold the QR code and the link will pop up.

Step 2: Once you enter your details an access link will be emailed to you.

Step 3: Either sign up through Hello Audio to download this private podcast to your favorite podcast platform, or listen to each episode on the Meet Your Colleagues website.

"The only real mistake is the one from which we learn nothing"
- Mason Cooley

Section Three

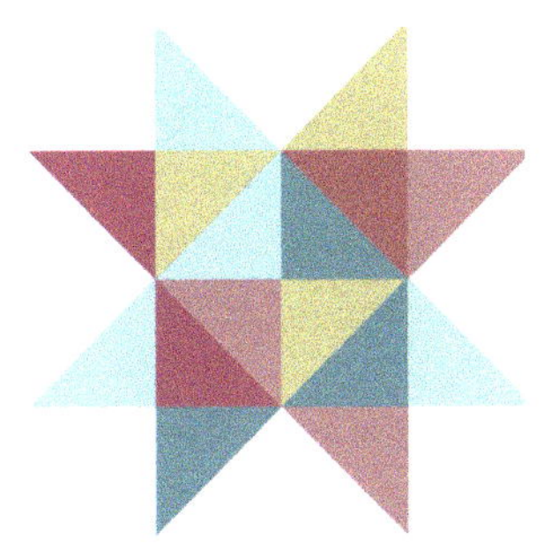

Elevate Your Workshop

Next Level Instruction

After you're comfortable with the content of your workshop, it's time to step it up to the next level. As workshop instructors, we're always seeking innovative ways to engage our students and create memorable experiences. To help create a next-level workshop your students need to have fun and feel safe to experiment and explore their creativity.

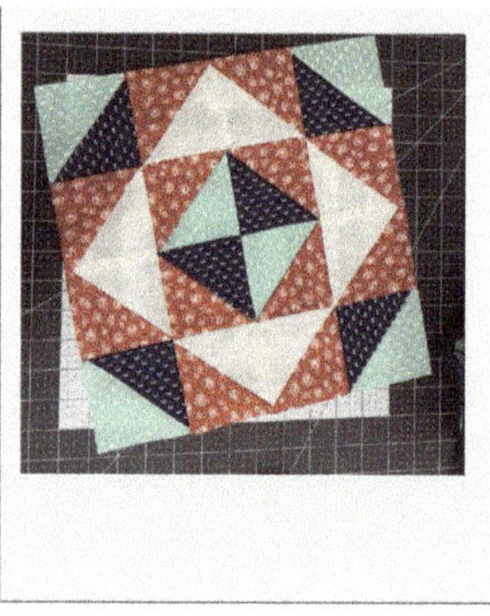

What better way to learn how to host an excellent experience than to look to a universally enjoyable event? A concert. Whether you're a metalhead (like my husband), a Taylor Swift Swiftie, or a part of Beyonce's BeyHive (all had amazing concerts in 2023!), there's much to glean from the dynamics of such high-energy events.

Surprise and Delight

Metallica and Taylor Swift concerts are renowned for their surprises—from unexpected song selections to guest appearances. Similarly, workshops can benefit from incorporating moments of surprise and delight. Consider introducing unexpected activities, guest speakers, or bonus materials to keep participants engaged and excited about what's to come. Like Taylor Swift always performing two songs that are different from any other concert, these elements will build anticipation. Embrace the unknown and allow participants to discover valuable insights as the workshop unfolds.

Presenting a technique that isn't immediately obvious can be really fun for both you and your students. If you're teaching a collage-style appliqué workshop, an English paper piecing workshop, or a pattern that incorporates a fun piecing technique—don't give away your process until your students are in the workshop with you. See how the mystery can build anticipation and enjoyment!

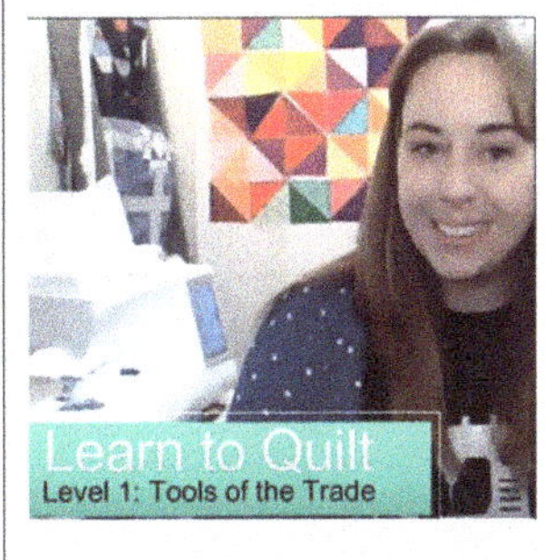

One way I've incorporated surprise and delight in my Level 1 Quilting Workshop was to have my students learn the burrito method of creating a pillowcase. Without fail, I would get comments like "Are you sure this is going to work?" and "I don't see how this is going to be a pillowcase." I would insist they trust the process, and without a doubt, they would smile or outright laugh when turning the burrito inside out to discover an almost complete pillowcase!

Lead with Fun and Enjoyment

Events, like concerts, epitomize the essence of fun and enjoyment. Similarly, workshops should be engaging and enjoyable experiences for students. Many students join workshops for the social aspect and *because it looks fun!* Infuse elements of playfulness and excitement into your workshops to foster a positive and dynamic learning environment. If it's not fun for you, it's certainly not going to be fun for your students.

How can we infuse more fun into a workshop? You, as the instructor and guide, have an amazing power to sway the energy in the room. Walk around, don't sit in one place, cheer them on, and have them share their progress. Tell stories when you can and when appropriate. You can use fun materials in your workshop examples, wear a crown so you're easy to find (great for large workshops at a quilt show), host your workshop at an unusual place, bring a fun snack—whatever you think can add some fun, try it out!

At any event, audience participation is key to the overall experience. Likewise, encourage active participation from workshop attendees through interactive activities, group discussions, and hands-on exercises.

Many concerts use a circular stage so the artist or band is able to move around and engage the audience all around the arena. Be sure you're using the same tactic by moving around within the room or on camera by changing angles and views. You can also engage participants who are quiet with questions, ask the opinion of those who have shared they have been quilting for a long time, and show how you have applied this skill to your pattern in real-world projects.

Again, don't sit in one place. If you're sewing alone and working on a project while students are working, your students will not feel seen, engaged, or very willing to ask questions. Walk around, socialize, observe, and compliment your students. Participate as much as you can to help them engage and fully participate in the workshop.

You can also add a little mystery to keep them guessing. A little bit of mystery automatically applies in many workshops simply because your students have come to learn. Keep workshop participants engaged by introducing unexpected challenges (within reason) or thought-provoking questions that spark curiosity and critical thinking.

When I taught free motion quilting, for example, I had students start with basic designs and gave them at least one challenging design to attempt before the workshop was over. They would look at me incredulously when I would introduce a design they considered out of their league because it looked way too complicated. However, by the end of our time together, they walked away with pride at their beautifully quilted sample square! It was physical proof of their achievement.

Offer Exclusive Merchandise and a Possible VIP Experience

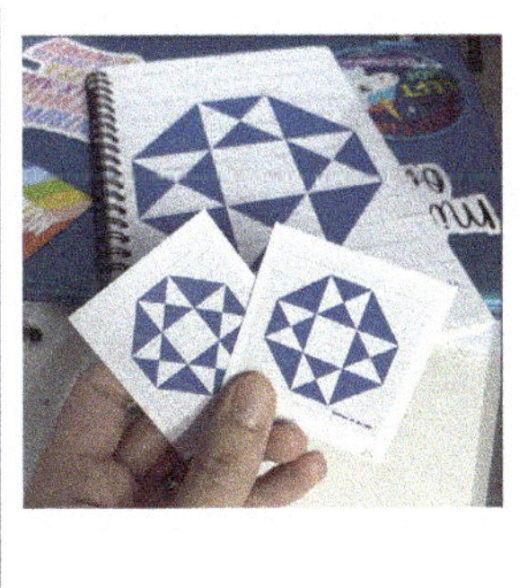

Metallica concerts often feature exclusive merchandise and special experiences for VIP ticket holders. Consider offering unique perks or bonuses for workshop participants, such as access to exclusive resources like tip sheets, expanded or exclusive patterns, access to a digital workshop, one-on-one or small group follow-up sessions, or early access to future events. Here, the lead guitarists riffed and created an exclusive song just for the night to enjoy! They then recorded the concert and sent all VIP Ticket holders a CD of the entire concert! What a great way to include exclusivity!

This is ideal for a larger workshop, one with many participants, one that covers multiple days, or a complicated technique workshop. If you're teaching online, this could look like tiered pricing and maybe even a goodie box for an event (think sewing retreat) that lasts a couple of days.

Involve the Local Community (for in-person workshops)

Metallica concerts often engage with local communities through charity initiatives or collaborations with local artists. Similarly, consider involving the local community in your workshops through partnerships, guest speakers, or supporting local businesses.

What could this look like to you, the instructor? If you're teaching for a shop or Quilt Guild, reach out to other local shops and Quilt Guilds to see if they'd like to book you as well. This could look like a book signing or pattern signing event set up at a quilt shop or even a local bookshop. Would you have the opportunity to be an in-person guest for a podcast or YouTube show?

Don't underestimate the power of advertising your in-person workshops to your email list and on social media. Be sure to tag the location when sharing on social media so the platform can share it with those who are local.

Incorporate Moments for Reflection and Recovery

Allowing students time to reflect can be quick and easy with an immensely valuable outcome. So many instructors go, go, go! Their pace is so fast that participants don’t get the chance to reflect on the information they’re learning.

Reflection is a powerful tool for helping your students feel like they have invested their time, energy, and finances wisely. Plus, it can be quick! Here's what happens when you grant them a few minutes of reflection:

1. **Reinforcement:** Reflecting on the skill, activity, or information presented in a workshop helps students reinforce their understanding of the content. By revisiting and

reviewing the key steps or concepts, attendees are more likely to remember what they learned.

2. **Application:** Reflection allows students to think about how they can apply the information learned in the workshop to their projects or how they can use their newly acquired skill in their next project. It helps them make connections between the workshop content and their real-life situations, enabling them to implement the knowledge effectively.

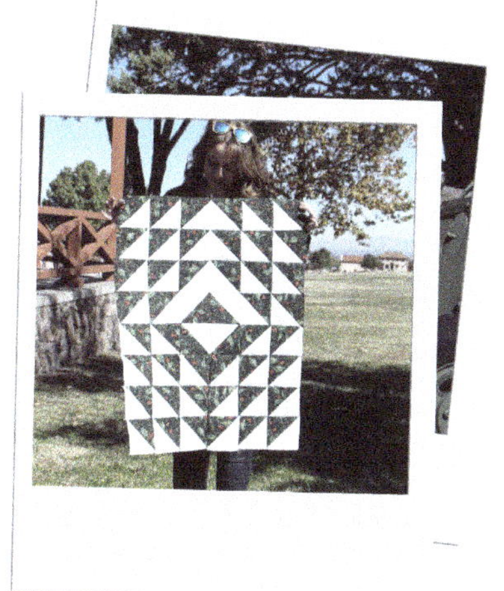

3. **Insight and Growth:** Reflecting on the workshop can provide students with valuable insights and new perspectives. It also allows them to review how their time, energy, and money were spent. It encourages critical thinking, self-awareness, and self-assessment. By considering how the workshop content relates to their own experiences, students can gain new insights and identify their success and areas for improvement.

How can you work reflection into a workshop? My favorite way is quick and gives you feedback at the same time: asking for Ah-ha Moments! Ask your students, "What ah-ha moments did you have today? What information, tip, etc. made you go 'Ah-ha! I get it now?'" As they take a few moments to share, they're reflecting on what they learned, seeing the value of their time and money, and you get feedback—it's a win, win, win!

However, there are many ways a teacher can add reflection opportunities during a workshop.

Individual Reflection

Allocate specific time during the workshop for participants to reflect individually on the information presented. This can be done through writing exercises, journaling, or self-assessment activities. Provide prompts or guiding questions to help participants focus their reflections.

Group Discussions

Facilitate group discussions where participants can share their thoughts, insights, and any questions about the workshop content. This is where the ah-ha moments come into play. Encourage active participation and create a safe and inclusive environment for open dialogue.

You can even assign group tasks or case studies that require collaborative reflection and problem-solving. For instance, when teaching about color, I had students do an activity called a Party Pull. I began with a colorful, bold print and each participant used the theories we learned in class to pull fabric to coordinate and build a fabric palette as a team. It took teamwork, discussion, and immediately put into practice the theories learned in the workshop allowing them to reflect.

Peer Feedback

Incorporate peer feedback sessions where participants can provide constructive feedback to each other. This can be done through structured feedback forms or guided discussions. Such as show and tell, where you can have individuals share their projects at the end or at specific points during the workshop. Encourage participants to reflect on each other's ideas, perspectives, and presentations, fostering a culture of learning from one another.

Reflection Prompts

Questions such as "How will you use this in your next project?" or "What will you be doing with your finished project?" provide students an opportunity to reflect on what they learned and how they will move forward using the skills or project they've created in the workshop. These can be given during the workshop or at the end.

Taking time to reflect is like the secret sauce for success in workshops. It's not just about learning; it's about feeling good about what you've learned and wanting to come back for more.

When students get the chance to reflect, it's not just a breather from the action; it's like hitting the pause button to let everything sink in. They have the opportunity to connect the dots, figure out where they're growing, and see how they can use what they've learned in their next project or how they will use the project completed for the workshop.

Reflection can also be sharing thoughts, bouncing ideas off each other, and feeling like part of a team. Whether chatting in groups, giving each other feedback, or just jotting down thoughts, it's about learning together and cheering each other on.

Reflection can help your students see and acknowledge their success. When they feel successful they come back for more—and they may even refer a friend!

Create a Safe Learning Space

I was so embarrassed; I just wanted to crawl under the table and hide. I had no idea what this instructor was talking about! I was around fourteen years old, accompanying my mom to a quilt class making a…I-don't-even-know-what table runner.

The instructor seemed like she was speaking a different language and seemed so frustrated and annoyed that I was even there. I didn't finish the project (my mom finished it to practice FMQ), but the same feelings of embarrassment and frustration fill me whenever I look at that table runner.

It fell out of the closet yesterday while searching for a backup toddler sheet set, and even now, seventeen-ish years later, those feelings are almost as strong as they were the day I stood in class.

I've been learning a lot about psychological safety and how it can be used inside a workshop.

In creative workshops, it's important that your students feel safe to be creative or it will be difficult for them to create, like it was for me.

How can we as instructors help create psychological safety so that our students can let their creativity out?

Here are 3 simple ways you can create an inclusive environment:

Introduce Yourself at the Beginning of Your Workshop

Let them know who they are trusting their time with. Share your background and your experience with the subject you're teaching. Give them some insight into your personality and maybe even share a fun short story that is relevant to the subject. When they know more about who you are the more comfortable they will feel in your workshop.

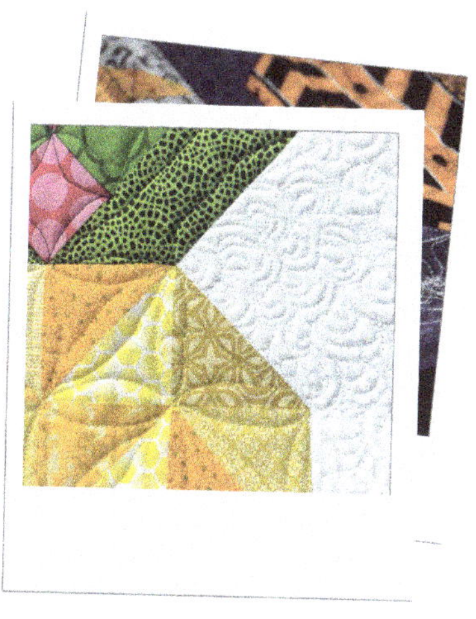

I loved to share how I was introduced to quilts. I was nine years old when I made my first quilt, so by the time I started teaching quilting, I had already been quilting for nineteen years! I always got a reaction when I began by letting them know how much time I had spent in this craft, despite being only twenty-eight years old. Then I would go into a story about when I started with the technique (especially if I struggled) or how I started designing patterns if I was teaching a pattern class.

As a reminder, you can keep this fairly short—about 5–7 minutes. You don't want to take too much time away from instruction, but it will help them get to know your expertise, building trust with your students and authority. They will then feel like they have made a good and safe investment of their time and money, and they'll be ready to learn! You can see more information about designing an introduction in the Design Your Workshop section.

Embrace Imperfections and Mistakes

Mistakes happen when you're teaching and that's okay! The projector won't turn on? The sewing machine is refusing to stay threaded? Did the needle break in the first fifteen minutes? Show your students you can keep your cool and forgive your own mistakes generously, and they will feel so much better about their own mistakes!

This will help create a safe environment for learning because when we're learning, we're making mistakes. In the quilting craft in particular, there is very little room for mistakes. Many quilters have been taught that perfection is the goal. This may be the case in competitions and shows, but in a workshop, mistakes are THE BEST way to learn. Help your students feel safe making mistakes by embracing your own and giving yourself grace.

Use Genuine Praise, Celebrate, and Thank Them for Sharing

Adults need praise and encouragement. We don't get enough. When you praise one student or thank them for sharing their work or their voice, the other students will feel safer sharing theirs!

When giving praise, be specific. Point out how they are taking risks and it's paying off. Point out their progress and celebrate it.

When teaching free motion quilting, I had so many students freeze up after putting their free motion quilting foot on their machine—too afraid to start. When they did, I celebrated! "You did it! You started! Now, it only gets easier from here." In that same class, they would have a practice square 12.5 in x 12.5 in, and by the time they quilted the same motif from one end to the next, they would make progress. You could see the pride shine through when I pointed it out. *Many students won't see the progress themselves until you point it out. Be their cheerleader!*

These small changes can make a big impact and leave a beautiful impression on your students.

They will feel safer, happier, and more successful in the workshop, and guess what? Successful students come back to learn more!

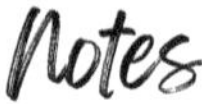

"People will forget what you said, people will forget what you did, but people will never forget how you made them feel"

\- **Maya Angelo**

Getting Valuable Feedback

"First, you are really passionate about what you do and are, therefore, a really good person to be a teacher. You are always available to answer questions, and your lessons are clear and easy to understand. Your smile always puts me in a good mood! Second, you really know your stuff, but welcome comments or suggestions from your students, making learning from you a real pleasure. Lastly, your pricing is really reasonable and affordable. I think you are worth every penny!!"

- Kelli Romanovsky, *Master Color Workshop*

As an instructor, keeping up with your audience and students is crucial to giving impactful and well-marketed workshops.

Not only do surveys give you insight into what can be improved on, but what you're doing great at. The quote above was from one of the first full workshops I taught! Notice that the quote highlights what I need to do more of in all of my workshops—including time for discussion, giving feedback quickly, and pricing for value not for time.

Also, when it comes to telling people about your workshop (marketing!), surveys are invaluable to finding your ideal customer and communicating the value of your workshop.

When to Get Feedback

I'd like to take you back to 2021. Quilt guilds are starting to meet in person again and I'm on stage in front of 80+ quilters sitting at large round tables around a community hall. There's a rainbow of colored fabric at each and every table. I'm teaching about color and having them sort their fabric by rainbow colors (reds, oranges, yellows, blues, greens, purples). Easy-peasy.

Then I explain the next step in the exercise: using the color wheel. The muttering starts...a few quilters reach hesitantly toward their new or gently used color wheels. The whispers turn into frustrated conversations and everyone is looking either bored or confused. I panicked, took a deep breath, set the microphone down, and stepped off the short stage.

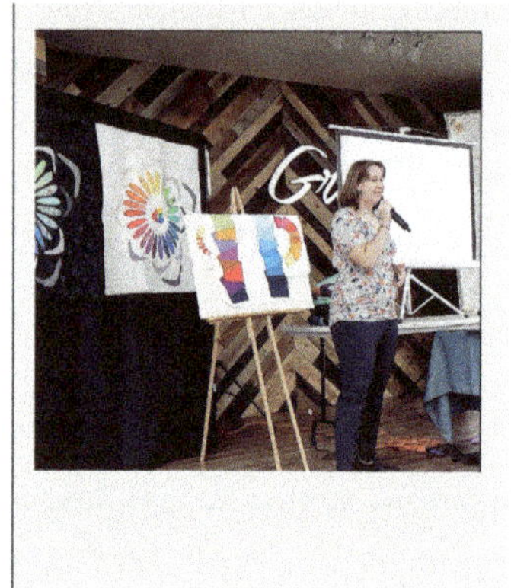

I visited every table in the hall, asked them where they were stuck, and re-explained the exercise. I quickly realized what was missing—they didn't know how a color wheel was supposed to be used. Their brains had turned off when I said the words “color wheel.” Many of them couldn't move past that and I wouldn't have known without feedback, without talking to them!

During your workshop, take moments to assess your attendees' progress and understanding simply by checking their facial expressions and asking "What questions do you have on (insert topic)?" or “Would you like me to demonstrate that again?” Avoid asking "Are there any questions?" Asking an open-ended question or offering to demonstrate steps again encourages more students to think about questions to ask. Most likely you will have one or two interruptions while you are redemonstrating and you can pinpoint where your students are confused or struggling.

At the end of the workshop, ask students if they had any "ah-ha" moments. As you may recall, this is my favorite way to have students reflect and ask for feedback! You could also ask what was their favorite topic or exercise they did during the workshop—something that excited them. This will provide wonderful feedback on what you are doing well and allow your attendees to reflect on what they learned—increasing the probability that their learning will stick. Not to mention, ending a workshop this way allows your students to feel more successful and like their time was spent well.

Another option is to hand out a physical survey at the end or near the end of the workshop. Make sure you tell them that there is a survey at the end of the workshop to prepare them to fill it out. I would suggest keeping this survey short by only including one to three of your most burning questions. Many students tend to hurry out at the end of a workshop, if your survey is too long they may not have time or even the energy to fill it out.

If you're teaching virtually, send them a survey directly after the workshop. If you are sending recordings or other supplemental materials, send the survey with that email as well. If your supplemental materials are hosted on a webpage, have a link to the survey there as well and remind them to take the survey. For your workshop to be successful, you need this feedback. Don't be afraid to ask them for their opinions.

I use the rule of three when asking for feedback. I ask my students to fill out a survey three times. Do not expect everyone to fill out a survey, it will not happen. However, if you let them know during the workshop that it's coming, that it's important to you, and you ask them to fill it out three times—whether that is in person or with three emails—you will get the feedback you need to see what's going well and what needs to be improved.

Before we get into my favorite questions, let's take a look at how to use different types of questions based on the responses you're looking for.

How to Use the List of Survey Questions

There's a fine balance between having a survey that is valuable and one that is short enough that your students don't mind taking the time to complete it. Start with the questions you want to know the answers to (2–3 questions). Then, build up from there.

Open questions (questions that require a unique response—not a one-word response or short phrase answer) are the most insightful, however, they do take time to fill out and you will get fewer (but more valuable!) responses.

Closed questions (one-word responses or short phrase response questions—like a rating scale or a yes/no question) are easy to fill out but do not leave room for elaboration. If you are looking for more responses rather than quality responses, closed questions are quick and easy to fill out and will generate more responses. These questions are great for quantifying or graphing responses and you will get more complete surveys.

So, which should you choose? I like to mix it up and make the closed, quick questions mandatory and the open questions optional.

Lastly, my beta offer, or the first time I launch a workshop, I offer it at a lower price but ask them to fill out a longer and more detailed survey. All learners who have attended a beta workshop have been happy to help fill out the survey for a lower price.

Not all these questions may apply or you may want to keep your surveys shorter. Feel free to pick what you'd like the most feedback on!

Real Feedback from the Master Color Workshop

The question was, "If you were to recommend this course to a friend, what would you say?"

The answers were as follows:

Student 1: *"You learn more than you think you will. It will help explain when a combination doesn't sit right and how to correct it."*

Student 2: *"That first, you are really passionate about what you do and are, therefore, a really good person to be a teacher. You are always available to answer questions and your lessons are clear and easy to understand. Your smile always puts me in a good mood! Second, you really know your stuff, but welcome comments or suggestions from your students, making learning from you a real pleasure. Last, your pricing is really reasonable and affordable. I think you are worth every penny!!"*

Student 3: *"It's great to learn and understand your color choices."*

Student 4: *"This class clarifies your understanding of color and helps you understand why sometimes the colors just aren't right and you can figure out how to fix it! I did that today! Also, you learn how to combine things. For example, which neutral to use with different color palettes, how different colors play together, and why some quilts sing and others are drab."*

There is so much value in this feedback! You can see their favorite parts and what they took away from the workshop, and where I may need to be more clear in my instruction. Their answers will help when sharing the value of the workshop, identifying where they struggled the most, and what problems the workshop solves (you can see more about how to use this in the Your Student's Journey section).

Survey Questions for Brand New Workshops (a.k.a. Beta Workshops)

Below are the added questions for longer follow-up surveys that I use for my brand-new workshops:

"Did you receive enough value for your time and expense?"

This question can give insight into how well you are communicating the value of the workshop.

"Were there any topics/concepts/steps that were confusing?"

Consider reworking these sections.

"How was the presentation? Could you hear and see the instructor and examples clearly?"

I use this question when my setup has changed.

Survey Questions for Established Workshops

"Did the Workshop meet your expectations? How? If not, what would you change?"

A GREAT question to help you analyze your communication in your marketing and description.

"What was most valuable?"

Feel free to format this question as a multiple-choice list or open question. This will give you insight on what to do more of AND what to focus on when you're marketing your workshop or workshops.

"Where did you hear about this workshop?"

Have you ever heard the marketing gurus say, "Share where your audience lives," or a form of that question? This answer gives great insight into where to focus your posts, shares, or marketing if you are marketing in multiple places.

"If you were to recommend this workshop to a friend, what would you say?"

Don't skip this one! This is the question that gives me stories, and impactful insight, and it gets them thinking about WHO would like this workshop and could inspire a recommendation to that person!

"Is there anything else you'd like me to know?"

This open question has been used in many ways. I have gotten feedback on parts of the experience that I hadn't considered asking about, stories, and another great place to get valuable testimonials to share on social media and marketing the workshop.

Ask permission to share their answers in the future marketing of the workshop.

It's always good to get their written expressed permission to use their words in your testimonials!

If I have a specific concern, I would add a specific question about it. So maybe a question about timing, or amount of follow-up emails after they signed up, etc.

Follow Up With Yourself

After every workshop, I set time aside to check out the survey answers. It can be a week after, twenty-four hours after I "close" the survey, or immediately after an in-person workshop. In a busy season, I have also waited to review the surveys until it's almost time to launch the workshop again. I don't suggest this, because sometimes there are questions in a survey that you have the opportunity to follow up on and create a great connection outside of the workshop.

Review the feedback, make a plan to apply what was shared that is relevant and useful, and document the testimonials for quick reference to make it easy for you to share on social media or for marketing the workshop.

As you grow, expect feedback from all directions. Remember to treat feedback as data—it's there to help you improve your workshops. However, setting healthy boundaries for your mental health is essential. If you encounter comments about things that are beyond your control or mean-spirited, dismiss them. You're not obligated to engage with feedback that lacks respect or comes from anyone who isn't a student. Focus on what matters, and let the rest go.

Be a Life-Long Learner

Go take a new workshop! Never stop learning. Learning something new is a wonderful way to expand your creativity and get fresh ideas on how to teach a craft. Take notes on how they're teaching you. Then take a few minutes to star or circle what you saw that was most effective for you and the way you learn. How was their time management? What did they offer after the workshop? How did they support your learning? What media did they use in the workshop (for example, prerecorded videos, slides, music, etc.) that were effective? Write it down.

Also, reflect on favorite workshops that you've taken in or outside of your craft. What did you love about them? What did the instructor do well? Write it all down. For your next workshop, take your observations and try one of those methods you enjoyed in your own workshop.

If you're looking to raise your prices, join a more expensive workshop. How did they design their workshop? Why did they charge more? Was it effective? Did the learners feel they got a great value for their time and expense? How was the instructor? Did they seem relaxed or excited? Were they nervous or exhausted? Observing the teacher can give you wonderful insights into the possibilities for your own business!

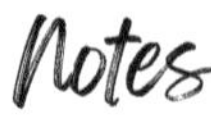

"Do not take feedback from any old body. We need to get selective about who we take feedback from."

-Rachel Rodgers

Section Four

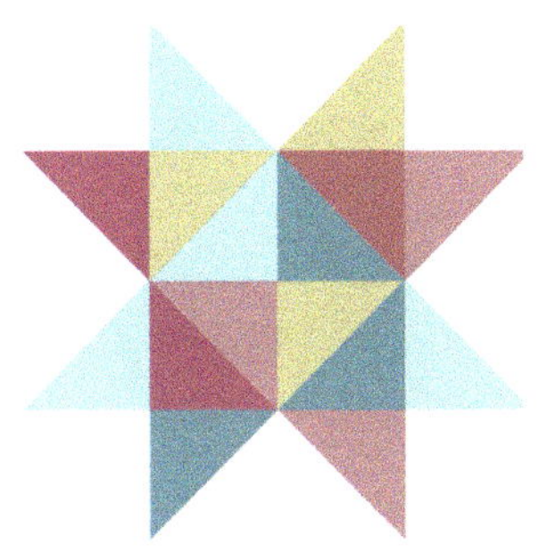

Your Students Journey

Your Student's Journey: A Holistic Way to Approach Workshop Marketing

You have your workshop ready to teach—excellent! The next step is to get butts in the seats—literally or virtually!

A Student's Journey is my simplistic and holistic way of creating an experience for students and it starts, as all marketing does, with your ideal student.

Who Is Your Ideal Student? An Exercise

You will want to dive deep into this description (I'll show you how to use this next). You may have a general idea of who your ideal student is, or you may need to take some time to reflect on the questions below.

If you're completely lost: go *find* your ideal student.

We have the gift of the internet, for better or for worse, every human you'd want to sell to uses the internet in some way, shape, or form. Social media is an excellent place to find your ideal student. Simply type into your favorite search engine your subject and the word "forum" or search your subject on your favorite social media platform and you'll find a wealth of information about your ideal student: who they are, what questions they are asking, what they are celebrating, and more! This is a simple form of market research. Don't stay stuck in your head—go out and find your ideal student.

If you're stuck, think about a past version of yourself. You can also use a past student or someone you know for inspiration, or combine several people into one customer.

The goal of this exercise is to get a good idea of who your students are, what they are looking for, what they do, where they hang out, and why they'd love your workshop.

- Who can you help the most? Who do *you* want to work with?
- What is this person's age, gender identity, and lifestyle?
- Where do they hang out virtually and in person?
- What are they struggling with right now?
- What do they want more of?
- What is the problem you solve with your instruction?

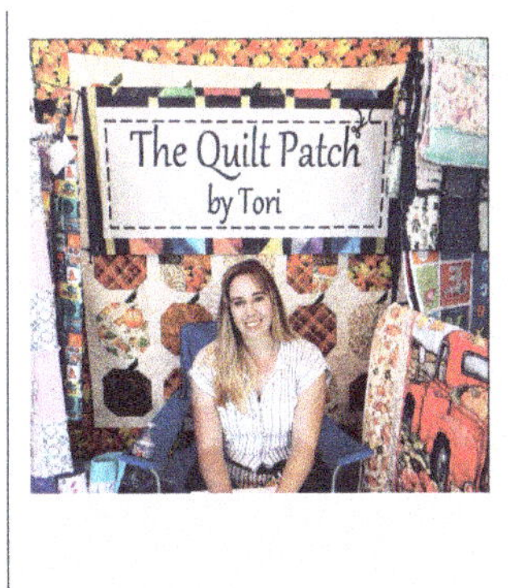

Then write them a biography based on all the information you have. Or ask AI to help you create an ideal student profile by dropping in the answers to the questions above. Be sure to give this person a name and create a realistic picture of this person in your mind, or go as far as to draw them or use AI to create a picture of this person. The more realistic the better. If you only have a vague idea, start with that vague idea and update your ideal customer as you go.

Throughout planning your student's journey, keep in mind that you are perceiving your business through the eyes of your student. As a student, you'd want to feel welcomed, prepared, and ready for the workshop before it starts, supported throughout the learning experience, and successful after the workshop ends.

Let's take a closer look at how to set up a successful Student Journey to help your students feel prepared and successful.

Step 1: Your ideal student discovers you and your workshop!

Step 2: They choose to sign up for your workshop.

Step 3: The workshop.

Step 4: The follow-up.

Step 5: Keeping in touch with an email newsletter.

Step 1: Your Ideal Student Discovers You and Your Workshop!

The Student's Journey begins when they first encounter you or information about your workshop. Using the information you've gathered to build an ideal student profile, you can predict where they are and how you can best show up to capture their attention.

When you shift your point of view to your student's point of view, how do you want them to begin their journey with you? How do you want them to feel before the class? How do they prepare? What do they need to know before they can be successful in the workshop?

The answers to these questions can lead to the content you share to draw your ideal student in.

For instance, if you're sharing a workshop teaching a beginner-friendly pattern that uses long straight seams, your students need to know how to sew a straight ¼-inch seam. Knowing this information, you can then write a blog post about perfecting the ¼-inch seam will attract beginner quilters looking to master that skill. Within that blog post, you can share information about your beginner-friendly pattern and workshop and invite them to purchase (or sign up).

There are many strategies for bringing your student in. You can see more about this in the Integrating Social Media section for more information.

Step 2: They Choose to Sign Up for Your Workshop

The second step for your student on the Student Journey happens right after they sign up for the workshop. What information do they need access to in order to prepare them for the workshop? If you are working with a third party, such as a quilt shop, guild, or show, you want to think through how the contact person will be able to get the information about the workshop prep to them.

If you're running an in-person or virtual workshop through your own event or system, this will be a lot easier. I would suggest using email to keep the processes simple, personable, and easy for them to access.

You will need to make sure they have all the materials they need (see the Materials section for more details) and the who, what, when, and where of the workshop so they can show up on time and ready to start. If this is a multi-day or multi-session workshop, consider putting together a syllabus that students can reference throughout the workshop that outlines the topics for each day, the materials for each session (especially if the materials change), and the days/times for each session. Make sure to include your contact information!

For prerecorded classes, this information should be included in the Introduction Module. More information about this is in the Resources section.

If you have multiple days leading up to a live or in-person workshop, and you're able to email your attendees, you can sprinkle inspiration emails in as well, to keep their excitement

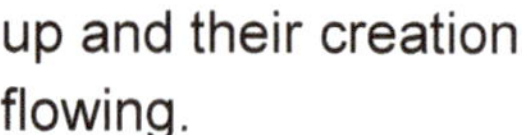

up and their creation flowing.

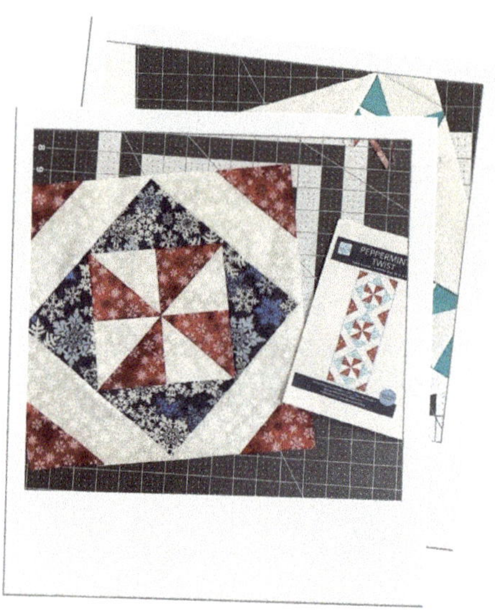

For instance, when I did my very first quilt-a-long, I decided to host a block-building workshop to kick it off. I released the pattern on day one and day ten was the workshop kick-off. I planned emails leading up to the workshop that showed digital images of the different colorway options, and how the quilt could look different depending on the size and the colors that the students chose. It helped build their excitement and inspired a few to change their color choices leading up to the workshop. This enthusiasm will also lead students to invite others to join the workshop and will increase how many people show up!

Step 3: The Workshop!

Because you have gone through and *designed* an impactful workshop throughout this book, this step in the Student's Journey will be easy and fun! You've explored how to clearly teach your topic, created an informative introduction, and included multiple ways to engage your students. Continue to excel and develop an excellent workshop experience and your students will come back for more, refer you as an instructor, and bring their friends!

If this is a prerecorded workshop they are going through, I highly recommend you include a live event or a series of live events where they can interact with you while they're working through the content. They need to know you are present and available to answer their questions. This could look like setting up an hour-long call with you or a weekly study hall hour where they can work with you in a small group or one-on-one. It could look like kicking off the prerecorded workshop with a live kickoff party, reiterating the introductory information. Then, as you release the individual lessons, you can set meeting times for Q&A until the course is complete.

There are so many ways for you to show up live and encourage your students to not only engage with the course material but to complete it.

Also, if this is an in-person workshop with a third party, it will be very important to ask for your participants' feedback and their email addresses at the workshop. No need to be pushy, but have a newsletter sign-up available and let them know how you plan to follow up with them after the workshop. Encourage them to sign up, remind them three times, and allow them to choose whether they'd like to stay in touch or not.

Step 4: The Follow-Up

The fourth step is the follow-up—what you do immediately after the workshop ends. Sending a personable email will be very beneficial for your participant. Include any links to resources, bonuses, and recordings from the workshop. This is also a great time to send a survey and let them know how they can get in touch with you moving forward.

The Power of the Follow-up

Following up with people is essential.

When I first began quilt pattern design, I took an eight-week course with a well-known pattern designer on how to start a business. It was intense and exciting. I showed up live to every class, coaching call, and Q&A, and I was active online with the group. I had a toddler at the time, so many days I'd have my headphones in, following him around with my worksheet, playing a little here and there while listening intently for the answers, filling out the exercises, and writing down notes and ideas. So much so, that my toddler learned how to hold a crayon and would "write" in his notebook while I was writing in mine! It was tough trying to care for him and design a business model, patterns, and workshops all at once, but I made it happen with a little creativity and tried to involve him as much as possible.

I still remember the adorable pride he had carrying around his notepad and scribbling like Mom. I also remember the fervor I approached this business with during those eight weeks. I built a website in the evenings and set up my first email list. I was not tech-savvy by any means, but I was so excited to have found a new direction after giving up on my lifelong pursuit of being a teacher in the public classroom that

I dived in and learned how to do it one step at a time. I was excited like I hadn't been in years about my future and I couldn't stop working.

But then everything came to a grinding stop.

We had a graduation party and poof! Everyone seemed to vanish. A few of us very dedicated students created a separate follow-up group to keep in touch and it lasted a few months, but after the graduation party, the excited and engaged community I had been a part of, the one that inspired and fueled my new dream, was gone.

Without our host we floundered. This particular course was launched again a year later, but I couldn't seem to find the same enthusiasm and encouragement in the new group as I did with the first. I knew that at the end, they'd all vanish and I couldn't bring myself to fully invest. It was discouraging and disheartening, and I did not learn as much.

Two years later I joined a community that did not have a singular course—it was an at-your-own-pace program with many live community events. I was hesitant because it was such a large monetary investment and I had no idea if I'd get the help I needed. What I found was a low-touch, but steady community with ongoing support. It wasn't fueled by excitement and fever; it was a slow-burn, built-to-last environment that had a strong foundation and leadership to support your growth. It was like a warm hug after a long, lonely time in my entrepreneurship journey.

When you dedicate so much time and energy into your workshops, and into your businesses, do not disappear on your students. You need to be present after the workshop, and you need to be consistent if you want to keep your business thriving. This is the basis for building a community around your business. This doesn't mean you need to run and set up a Facebook Group, but I would strongly suggest that if you're looking for growth and long-term success, you need to be consistently showing up in front of your future, current, and past students. Determine what consistency means for you and your bandwidth and stick to it. What can this look like?

You can go full force with a free and/or paid membership, where you host follow-up training, discussions, and events, or you can simplify how you show up by emailing a newsletter every week or two to send updates, inspiration, and tips. Figure out where you fall on this pendulum of community building and involvement and be consistent.

What happens if you completely disappear after a student finishes your course?

You lose momentum with that student. Your student loses momentum, and they are less likely to purchase from you or refer your workshop to others in the future. This forces you to fight an uphill battle every time you open sign-ups for the next workshop or whenever you launch a new one. You'll have to start from scratch every time you want a student to sign up for a workshop. It takes a lot more energy to get a ball rolling than it does to keep a ball rolling, and something as simple as a biweekly newsletter can gently keep the ball rolling so you never lose all your momentum.

Step 5: Keep in Touch with an Email Newsletter

The Power of the Email List

In today's digital age, where social media platforms dominate our online interactions, it's easy to overlook the quiet champion of enduring effectiveness—email. As a quilting or crafting workshop instructor, cultivating an engaged email list can be a game-changer for filling your workshops and expanding your audience. There are many benefits of email communication. Let's look at how to start an email list and the importance of newsletters in engaging your subscribers.

The Power of Email for Marketing Your Workshop

Firstly, let's highlight the superiority of email communication over social media. Email messages go straight to your audience's inbox. It's a place they curate. It is not made to distract like social media. What's even more powerful is open rates (the percentage of people who open and view your email) and how many people will see the value you are offering in your email messages and in your workshops. Open rates are much higher than views on social media.

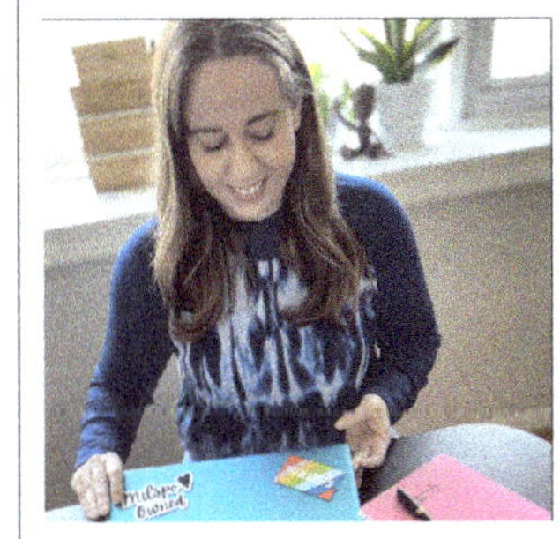

The Crafting Industry has an average open rate of 15–25%. However, keep in mind that the crafting community tends to have a highly engaged and passionate audience—because we love what we do! This can positively impact open rates as subscribers are genuinely interested in receiving relevant emails related to their craft *from you*. Focusing on quality content (there are ideas below) can increase these open rates dramatically.

Personally, my average open rate ranges from 41–47%, compared to the meager 2–10% reach of social media (unless you go viral, but that's not the norm). The industry average, at its low end, is 15%! That's still much better than average views on social media. In addition, email offers a more direct and reliable way to connect with your audience. You can be personable and give value without wasting a ton of energy on posts that only 2–10% of your followers will even see.

Specifically, for quilting or crafting instructors, email also makes signing up for a workshop so much easier. You can put a link right in the email that takes them straight to the checkout page. Your potential attendees won't have to go searching for the "link in bio." It's easy! And when it's easy, you will get many more attendees to follow through on booking the workshop.

By utilizing email, you can effectively communicate with your existing workshop attendees, nurture potential participants, and build a community. Let's dive into how we can make this happen.

Starting Your Email List

To embark on your email marketing journey, the first step is to choose a suitable Email Service Provider (ESP). Think of it as finding the perfect color thread for your quilt, or the perfect canvas for your next painting. Do a quick Google search and choose a few of the top suggestions. You can also ask for referrals from other businesses and quilting or crafting groups to see which they prefer. Then explore different ESPs, comparing features, rates (many are free up to a certain number of subscribers), automation capabilities, and the icing on the cake—landing pages. Landing pages are especially important if you don't have a website yet. This is a page where you can direct your audience to sign up for your email list. Start with a free version to get comfortable and see if it's easy for you to use before leveling up as your list grows.

Here's a short list for you to recap. You want to look at:

1. Price point
2. Automation (sending email messages automatically)
3. Landing pages
4. Ease of use—use the free version to find out
5. Consider aesthetics—does it match your brand?

Start Growing by Asking

Newsletters are a crucial component of your email marketing strategy. It's important to plan and structure your newsletters in a personable and fun way to capture your subscribers' interest and keep them engaged. Below are some tips to consider.

When you have chosen your ESP, the next thing to do is to set up a landing page where you can send subscribers to your email list. Then, ask your network (in person, on social media, or anyone you know) to sign up for your email list. Just start by asking and making your audience aware that you are beginning to offer a newsletter through your email list if they'd like to see more from you.

Set up an automated email to respond to and welcome each new subscriber. When someone signs up for your email list, you can seize the opportunity to learn more about their interests and preferences. Incorporate a brief survey or ask a simple question to understand what content they would like to receive from you. (Not ready for this yet? No worries! Just welcome new subscribers in every newsletter to help them feel more welcome.)

Crafting Engaging Newsletters

Next up is the all-important emailed newsletter.

You can keep this simple! Write like you're talking to a friend. My most successful emails are those that have notes about what I'm up to and contain genuine questions that my audience can respond to. Imagine sitting around a social circle, sipping tea or coffee, and swapping stories. Treat your subscribers like a good friend, asking them about their preferences and interests. This helps you tailor your content and make them feel valued and happy to engage with you.

I would invite you to make a plan for success. You need a roadmap for your newsletters. Create a template and a simple content calendar that brings structure and excitement. Share your expertise, what you're working on now, student work from past workshops, what's inspiring you now, and what your favorite quilting or crafting peers are also working on (or invite them to write for your newsletter!). Sprinkle in tips and tutorials, and announce upcoming workshops with a touch of anticipation.

Pick two to four things to share in each newsletter and end it with a major call to action. Are they listening to your podcast? Taking advantage of a deal? Sharing your newsletter with a friend for inspiration? Are they signing up for your next workshop? Decide ahead of time what you want them to do and then tell them what to do.

Keep in mind that consistency is key, and by planning ahead, you can deliver valuable content without feeling overwhelmed. I find many entrepreneurs are hesitant to email too much and choose to email once a month or when they are promoting something. I'm here to say that it's not enough. Your subscribers will forget you. I started writing my newsletter every two weeks or twice a month, and my unsubscribe rate dropped dramatically. My subscribers remember me much better and it keeps my workshops and blog resources top of mind. Ideally, I would be sending a newsletter once a week. I'll get there soon!

Integrating Social Media

While email reigns supreme, social media works together with the intimacy of email as a complementary tool to enhance your reach and engagement. Utilize your email list to promote your social media accounts and encourage subscribers to follow and engage with you there. This helps keep you and your workshops top of mind. Likewise, use social media to capture new leads for your email list by providing incentives such as exclusive content, challenges or events, a freebie, or giveaways for signing up.

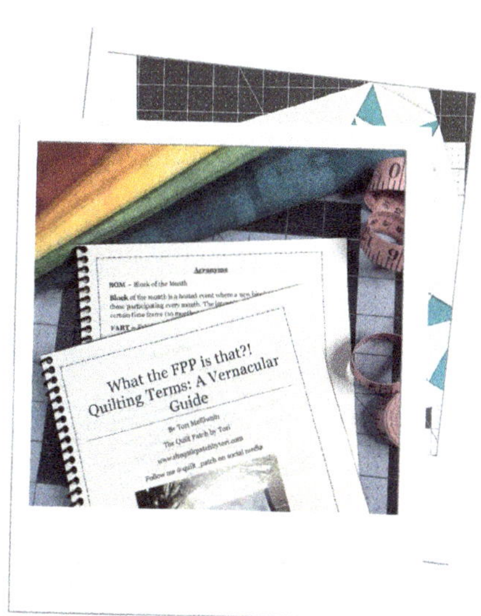

It sounds like a lot of work, but following the steps above and having a template that you can plug information into every week (yes, weekly is the goal remember?) will create a process that you can move through with ease and fun!

In the world of creative workshops, email remains the most effective method of communication for instructors. By building an email list and crafting engaging newsletters, you can successfully fill your workshops and foster a thriving community. Remember to prioritize your audience's preferences, invest in a reliable email service provider, and leverage the power of social media to maximize your impact. Embrace the potential of email marketing and watch your workshops flourish like never before.

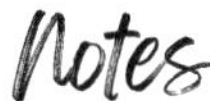

"Put one foot in front of the other, focus on the little goal right in front of you, and almost anything is possible."

\- **Joe De Sena**

Launching

Launching is a digital marketing strategy. It's the process of turning your workshop into an event. You can use the Launch Strategy to draw your ideal student in through email, social media, and more. You want your students to feel prepared and excited to attend the workshop, as well as ready to learn and create with you.

I grew up next to Edwards Air Force Base in California, and when I learned about what a Launch Strategy was I couldn't help but recall the literal rocket launches I witnessed growing up. My teachers would always work in lessons about rockets into our classroom curriculum, and it built the understanding about what was going to happen and increased excitement! We had coloring sheets about rockets, we watched videos about them, we got familiar with the different terminology used when discussing launching a rocket, we learned the different parts and what they were used for, and more! That's exactly what you want to do with a workshop launch.

If you choose to use the Launch Strategy you want to educate, inspire, and generate excitement about your workshop!

Let's compare launching a workshop to the launch of a rocket into space. In order for the launch to be successful, so many things have to happen before the day of the launch, also known as the Cart Open Day or the day you open registration for your workshop. Although I don't know the ins and outs of planning for an actual rocket launch, I've experienced and observed the prep that goes into preparing for a workshop launch. We need to prepare the site, the crew (you!), and your community—much like a rocket launch.

To prep the site, you need to set up a waitlist, create a landing page, and offer a freebie to entice potential participants. The waitlist allows interested individuals to sign up in advance and ensures you have a list of eager participants ready to go when registration opens. The landing page provides information about the workshop, its benefits, and a call to action to join the waitlist. Finally, offering a freebie, such as a downloadable resource or mini-training, can help build anticipation and provide a taste of what participants can expect from the workshop.

Prepping the crew is essential for a successful workshop launch. This involves getting your mindset straight and gathering support. It's important to have a clear vision for your workshop and align your mindset with success. Surrounding yourself with a supportive network, whether it's friends, family, or fellow entrepreneurs, can provide encouragement, advice, and accountability during the launch process.

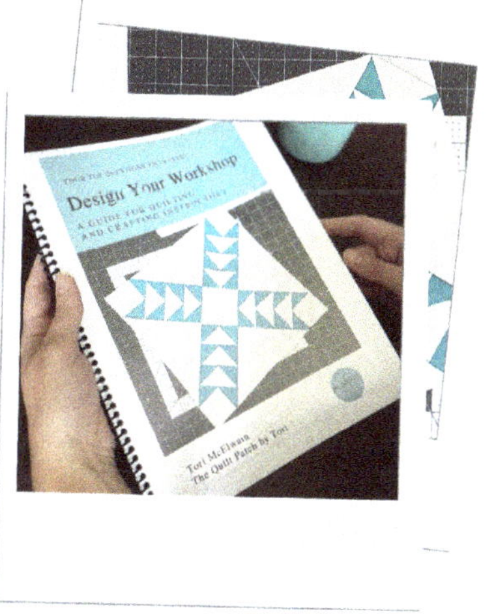

Preparing the community is another crucial step. You want to get everyone ready and excited for the workshop. Consider hosting a free event or an email series leading up to the launch. This allows you to provide value, showcase your expertise, and generate interest among your target audience. By engaging with your community before the launch, you can build trust and anticipation, increasing the likelihood of a successful workshop launch.

Remember, just like a rocket launch, proper preparation is key to a successful workshop launch. By prepping the site, crew, and community, you can set yourself up for a smooth and impactful launch day.

Then, the countdown begins. All content created for 2–3 weeks before Cart Open Day can generate interest.

Keep in mind these two key questions:

1. What do they need to know to be prepared for the workshop?

2. How are they feeling before your workshop, and how do you want them to feel after your workshop?

The timing can vary depending on what you're offering. If this is a multi-day workshop or a higher-priced workshop, you may need to build up your audience's trust a little more before Open Cart Day.

Choose a date for your Open Cart Day. Typically, this will be 5–7 days before you have your workshop or open your prerecorded workshop for new students. Choose a timeline for your launch between three weeks to ten days, and start sharing! Below you'll find a 10-day countdown and suggested content for your emails and social media.

Before the launch officially kicks off, spend time brainstorming ideas for content. Answer the following questions or use your notes from the Objective section:

- Who is this workshop for?

- What is the skill level?

- What skills do they need before they join the workshop?
- What questions do they have about your topic?
- What are they struggling with [topic]?
- What mistakes are they making, and how can your workshop help?
- What are some myths or misconceptions around your topic that you could dispel?
- What are ways you can cultivate curiosity?

The answers to these questions can help you create content to share in your emails, social media posts, and any core content such as blogs, podcasts, YouTube videos, etc. As you lead up to the Launch Sequence outline below, share content that answers the questions above. You'll notice that the longer you share content like this to attract your ideal students, the more trust and authority you will build with your audience.

As a reminder, the content you share and the timing can be different as you lead up to Open Cart Day. You can also schedule much, if not all, of this in advance. Choose a schedule of sharing and publishing that works for you. My strongest suggestion is to stick to the Open Cart Email Sequence in the suggested timeline below.

The Countdown Begins

...Day 10...Send out a simple email asking your audience one question, "What top two things do I need to cover/include/ in [your workshop]." This is the kick-off to the launch that Jeff Walker describes in detail in his book, *Launch*. I have used this start for years and love the feedback I get! Post this on social media as well.

...Day 9...Take note of the feedback coming in, whether it's one answer or one hundred. The feedback from this survey can help with refining your workshop and help your audience feel that they are involved in creating it.

...Day 8...Evaluate your feedback and take action where needed. Adjust your wording, possibly even adjust your workshop, as needed.

...Day 7...Send out your weekly newsletter and include a thank you to your audience for answering the survey, and feel free to share some of the information you gathered. Within that email, announce your workshop with your carefully prepared description (see more about this in the Objective section). Let your audience know that there is a waitlist available for your upcoming workshop. Share that same information with a post or two on social media.

...Day 6, 5, 4...Share content on social media that addresses any myths, misconceptions, and objections. Some common misconceptions when it comes to quilting techniques are the time they may take and the difficulty of the different skills, patterns, or techniques.

...Day 3...(optional) Send a short email to your waitlist reminding them that registration opens in just 3 days! Include some inspiration or behind-the-scenes footage. Share a shortened version on social media as well.

...Day 2...Send a short email to your waitlist to remind them that registration opens in just forty-eight hours! Share on social media as well.

...Day 1! Open Cart Day!

Open Cart Email Sequence: The lift-off!

Open Cart Day 1: Send an email invitation to sign up for your workshop—registration is open! Include the description and the transformation you are providing with the workshop. Remind them when the cart will close as well. Post two times on social media sharing the same information.

Open Cart Day 2: Send an email answering their questions or dispel some myths about your workshop's topic. Post two times on social media sharing the same information.

Open Cart Day 3: Send an email detailing the transformation that they will get with the workshop. Include 3–4 testimonials if you have them! Post the testimonials on social media sharing the same information.

Open Cart Day 4: The day before closing day, your email is really speaking to anyone who may be on the fence about joining you for this workshop. Share a story of transformation whether it's yours or a student's. Tell a story to help them picture how this skill will help them or this project will add value to their life.

Cart Closing Day: Send 3 emails on Cart Closing Day.

1. The morning email: This is the last chance email. Answer the top three frequently asked questions you've gotten. I also like to include a countdown timer if available with your email service provider.

2. The afternoon email: Emphasize why they need to take action now (the problem could be solved, the cart will close tonight, etc.)

3. Six Hours before closing: Final call email. Keep this one short and sweet with a very clear call to action.

The cart is now closed and the workshop is about to begin! The rocket has lifted off and the mission has started; take the stage, the front of the classroom, or turn on the camera, it's time to introduce yourself!

One last email for your audience members who did not purchase: Ask them why they chose not to join this time, and invite them to access your free content on social media or any other low-cost resources you provide for your audience. As mentioned previously, you don't want to disappear from your audience after they followed you throughout the launch. After all, they may not be ready to purchase now, but they may be ready the next time you launch.

As you have seen, a Launch is a digital marketing strategy. However, it can also be used with some tweaks for an in-person workshop. Even if your workshop is in person and takes place at a venue like a guild meeting or shop where you don't have full control, this information can still be valuable.

Share about the workshop on social media (being sure to tag the venue or city) and with your email list, letting them know you will be teaching locally, and share some helpful information leading up to the workshop. Just because this is in person and not available to your whole email list or followers/subscribers doesn't mean a few wouldn't love to join! You might even receive some referrals to other local Quilt Guilds or quilt shops for you to teach in their area, teach an online class, or give them access to a recorded workshop. So, in short, share everywhere because you never know what other opportunities may arise.

Between launches, keep your audience warm with your weekly or biweekly newsletters!

Marketing as a whole is experimentation. My biggest piece of advice when you are marketing a workshop is to get to know your ideal student *the best*, show up where they are—online or in person—and communicate in a way that feels most authentic to you. Make it fun and your ideal student is going to feel that energy!

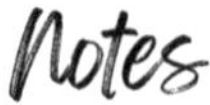

"Don't sit down and wait for the opportunities to come. Get up and make them"

- **Madam C. J. Walker**

Programs

Programs, also called lectures, or online are referred to as webinars, are presentations that last anywhere from forty-five minutes to an hour and thirty minutes. They are presented to a community of crafters. Many craft guilds love to invite teachers in to demonstrate, inspire, and teach their community more about the craft they love. There are many types of craft guilds throughout the world, from yarn guilds to quilting guilds and beyond. I have worked mainly with Quilt Guilds and hosted my own webinars, so in this section, I will use Quilt Guilds as an example, however, this format can work with any community presentation you'd like to host.

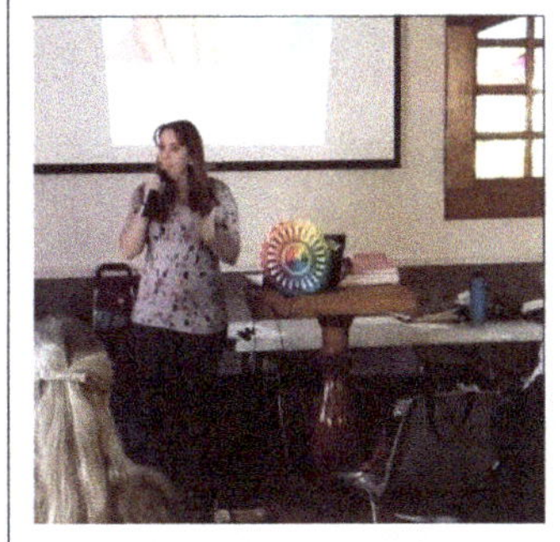

In the quilting industry, like in many other craft industries, guilds tend to be non-profit organizations built around community and quilting. Not all guilds are structured the same, but the majority are established to support their members and to do charitable work. Quilt Guilds will hire a teacher to give a lecture for an hour at their monthly meeting and typically book a follow-up half-day or full-day workshop with that same teacher. This allows their Guild to generate interest and give value to their members at the lecture, then raise funds for their Guild by charging for the workshop. As mentioned previously, not all guilds are designed the same way. Many Guilds are hoping to raise engagement rather than funds by hosting the workshop. Either way, you are teaming up with the guild leadership to encourage members to attend your main offer: the workshop.

You'll be able to do that with a well-structured and entertaining or inspiring program.

Programs can also be used as a webinar—an online presentation, paid or free, that you offer to your audience to give value, inspire, teach, and move your audience to your main offer: your workshop! It has the same end goal as the guild program.

Programs in either case are a great way to introduce yourself, build authority and trust, and present the content you teach to a large audience. It also is a great opportunity for you to generate more interest in your patterns, techniques, books, network, build relationships, travel, and generate some extra revenue!

The Who, What, Why and How

The second program I designed was about Movement in Quilting. I love quilts that allow your eyes to move around the design in different ways, such as diagonal lines or vines that snake around the edges of a quilt, allowing your eyes to travel up and around with the design. I had not heard of any other teacher or designer speaking about this concept and I was so excited to design a program around it. This particular program was designed in 2021, when almost all guilds were still only meeting virtually. I had reached out to my community of quilt pattern designers and my favorite long-arm quilter for samples of movement in quitting. I had broken the concept down to four main parts and gathered 70+ slides of examples. I listed it on my website and started sharing about it on social media.

The first time I presented this gigantic program to a guild, I was so nervous. I had only been able to practice it once and barely made it within an hour, but I was sure they'd want to see every example I was able to gather and would be just as excited as I was to learn about movement in quilting. The comments and feedback I received were (in all caps) "SO MUCH INFORMATION," and "Wow! That was a lot!" It was entirely too much. I had over delivered to the point that I had overwhelmed and confused my audience. The Guild ended up having to cancel the follow-up workshop due to a lack of sign-ups and I didn't hear from any of their 45+ members again.

A lost opportunity—but one you don't have to repeat!

The goal of a program is to teach your audience the "who," "what," and "why," and save all or most of the "how" for the paid workshop. You may want to include a little of the "how" to demonstrate a particularly challenging technique, but for the most part, instruction needs to be kept to the workshop. If you are trying to teach too much in forty-five minutes, within an hour you will overwhelm and confuse your audience as I did!

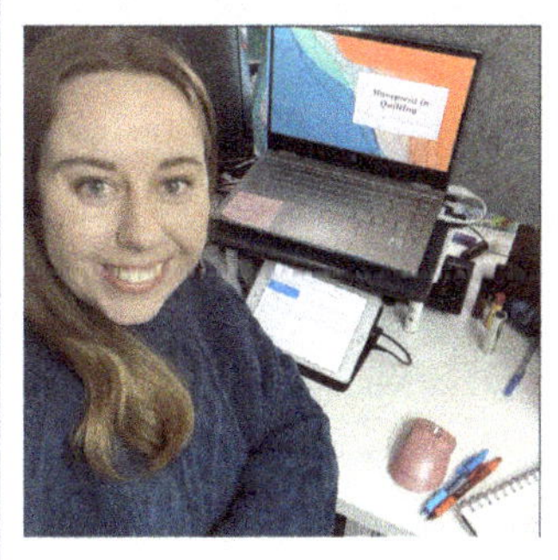

The "who" refers to you and who the pattern, technique, and skill set you teach is for. The "what" and "why" refer to the topic you're teaching. So essentially, your program will need to address the following questions:

- Who are you?
- What are you teaching?
- How do you teach?

- Who is this [topic] for? Beginners, advanced crafters, niched technique enthusiasts...?
- What do I do with this [topic] after I learn it?
- What can it be used for?
- Why do I, as a quilter [or insert your crafter], want to learn about this? What problem does it solve?

The answers to these questions are important for building trust, authority, and interest. It is important to give value and not fluff. The workshop is where your audience can get the most value out of what you teach, so save the step-by-step process where you can support your students for the workshop. With a workshop as your main offer, what you want to do is gain interest in the topic, skill, or patterns that you want to teach. You will want to show your teaching style, so pick between three and five points that you can teach that also do not overwhelm your audience in an hour.

Program Frameworks

There are many ways to structure a program. I've outlined two effective ways to structure a guild program to help get you started.

In the first framework, you lead with the teaching for about 20–25 minutes and use the rest of your time for examples. This can be a great structure for pattern designers.

- Teaching point 1:
    - 2–3 examples that showcase teaching point 1
- Teaching point 2:
    - 2–3 examples that showcase teaching point 2
- Teaching Point 3:
    - 2–3 examples that showcase teaching point 3
- Teaching point 4:

    - 2–3 examples that showcase teaching point 4
- 9–12 examples that showcase all four teaching points.

The numbers in this framework are significant. Notice that a total of fifteen examples can make a full program. Providing two to three examples while teaching gives your students a digestible number but also allows a little compare and contrast without feeling overwhelmed. The nine to twelve examples at the end are also digestible amounts for your audience. You can test out what feels comfortable to your audience and adjust the number of examples accordingly.

The second framework allows you to build on a concept or a topic. This can be a great framework for a technique or theory (such as color or design). It looks like this:

- Teaching Point 1:
    - 2–3 examples
- Teaching Point 2:
    - Two examples of Teaching Point 2
    - 2–3 example quilts that showcase the first two teaching points
- Teaching Point 3:
    - Two examples of Teaching Point 3
    - 2–3 example quilts that showcase the first three teaching points
- Teaching Point 4:
    - Two examples of Teaching Point 4
    - 2–3 example quilts that showcase all teaching points

See the full framework examples in the Resources section.

The Crafter's Journey

Everyone who has ever made a craft more than a handful of times has a crafter's journey. You can start presenting to groups with this Trunk Show style program if you are uncertain of any topic you'd like to teach.

In a Trunk Show, you're sharing your work—pulling examples from a literal or imagined traveling trunk. Many presenters will use this style of presentation for inspiration and use those examples to share their journey with a lesson. The lesson—teaching points—are key here. The biggest complaints I've heard from Guilds are about teachers who only showcase their work and do not spend any time teaching. What was the biggest lesson you learned while learning and growing your skillset?

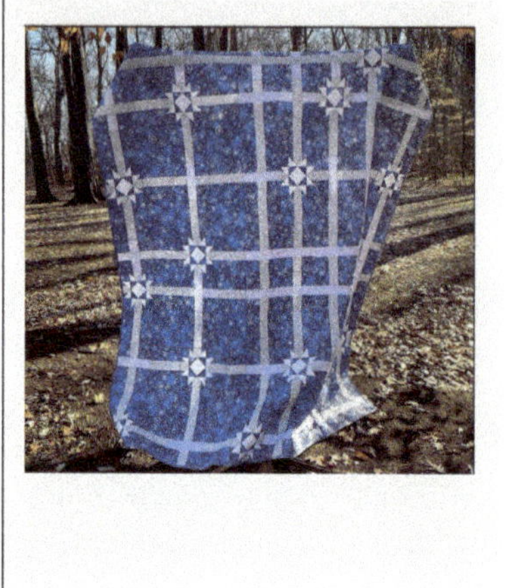

The lesson is the value you're going to give to your audience, and you can use that lesson to design your teaching points. Then use your craft as examples, inspiration, and teaching points. As a pattern designer who hosts workshops about their patterns, this can look like how you've developed your patterns and your skills throughout your quilting journey while showcasing your most popular patterns. You can mention the name of the pattern and that it is one designed by you, and then move into why you've chosen this example to demonstrate the teaching point. This way you can showcase the pattern, still deliver some great value for your audience, and at the very end, you can share where to find your workshops.

For instance, at the time I was presenting my Movement in Quilting Program, I was also offering live online color workshops. I would present a particular quilt as an example of how to use color to create movement and would casually mention, "In the color workshops that I teach, I go into more depth on how to use color for different effects. Today, I want to specify how I used color in this quilt to give it movement." It's a mention, but it's enough to pique a quilter's interest if they're interested in learning more about color.

When can you sell? Throughout this presentation, you will be sprinkling in tidbits about what you offer—like a ninja! Then at the very end of the presentation, they have already heard what you offer and you can just share where they can find it.

Here is the tail end of the Program Outline that lays out how you can end this type of presentation:

- Summarize your Teaching Points
- Lead a discussion or reflection
- Conclusion (approx. 5 minutes):
    - Share what you offer (patterns, workshops, services, etc.) and ONE way to access it (this can be your website or landing page)
    - Share ONE way to keep in touch with you (typically your main social media account or your email list)
    - Share a little about what you've brought with you today to sell (if applicable)
    - Ask for questions or invite them to speak to you after the presentation, and thank the group for hosting.

If you end by reminding them of the value you have provided and allow them time to commit to memory with a discussion or reflection, they will be more likely to hear about what else you offer. Keep it simple, short, and to the point without too many things to do. If you give them too many things to do you may cause confusion.

One last note on presentations and the Crafter's Journey Trunk Show: have *fun*. Show your skill off a bit—it's your time to show your personality, your style of quilting, and your creative journey. Don't be afraid to share your beginner work either. As discussed in the Elevate Your Workshop section, sharing your mistakes, your learning moments, or your less-than-favorable outcomes creates an environment of trust and acceptability. They will see you as a teacher they can learn from and who can lead them through their own learning mistakes.

Getting Started with Guilds

This is a frequently asked question in many crafting circles. Let's address how you can get started with guilds.

After you've designed your program, start local and start with a discount. If you are part of a guild or a similar community that likes to bring in teachers, let them know that you have designed a program and would like to offer a discount as a first-time presenter. Some offer up to 50% off.

Pricing can differ by experience, format, and skill level. Ask your fellow professionals how much they are charging for their programs. Many teachers who offer programs will also have their prices listed on their websites. As this book is being written in 2024, the average for a new presenter is between $300 and $350 for a forty-five-minute to an hour and fifteen-minute program. Typically, guilds will also book you for a follow-up workshop.

After your first program, start reaching out to guild representatives. The role you're looking for is the Guild Program Chair or Officer. You can cold email them a simple email and let them know where they can see more information about your program(s). You can also list your program on your website if you have one set up. If you choose to present your program virtually, you can also reach out to organizations such as the Global Quilt Connection and the Global Craft Connection.

Side Note

Why not present for free? We are pricing to thrive. You've spent years, decades, or at least some hard-earned time developing these skills and examples. Offering your knowledge for free is great in a social environment, but if you are getting serious about reaching a larger audience, building up a teaching business, and spending all the time, energy, and money it takes to design a program, I hope you charge for it—even at a discount. If I haven't convinced you to charge yet, I implore you to, at the very least, require feedback from those in attendance.

Look for different opportunities to share that you are looking for guilds. Many guilds will book six months to a year in advance, so be sure to have a simple contract, a calendar, and reminders set up so you're prepared when they start booking!

Time to Unleash Your Knowledge

You now have the tools, knowledge, and resources you need to create a wonderful learning experience. It's time to put this into action. If you've read straight through this book without pausing to do the exercises, go back and *do the work.* Taking time to really think through your workshop, class, or course is going to save you a ton of time, energy, and money.

Experience is the next thing you need to gather. Teach, take classes from others, and enjoy your teaching journey. It's then my hope that you share your enjoyment about your craft with your friends and family, your community, and throughout the world. You have an amazing skill that many people around the world would love to learn. You do not need certifications. You do not need to be the expert of all experts. You only need a little experience and the *want* to share what you've learned with others.

I cannot wait to see the lives you impact! You can spark creativity and joy in others whenever you share *your* creativity and joy!

Also, take the process of designing a workshop as slow or as fast as you need to. Designing an impactful workshop is a process of continuous improvement. Find support through this journey, we can not do this alone. Attend events, join communities of business-minded crafty entrepreneurs, and reach out to teachers with more experience for mentorship, accountability, and fun! Crafting instructors are some of the best people I've ever met. They're a warm, excitable and, of course, creative group of people!

Keep in mind: Your workshop will change, the subject will change, the drive and excitement will change, and even the way you teach will change. Follow your excitement, your curiosity, your creativity, and enjoy the ride!

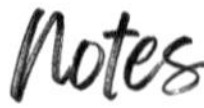

"Our deepest fear is not that we are inadequate. Our deepest fear is that we are powerful beyond measure."

- **Marianne Williamson**

Section Five

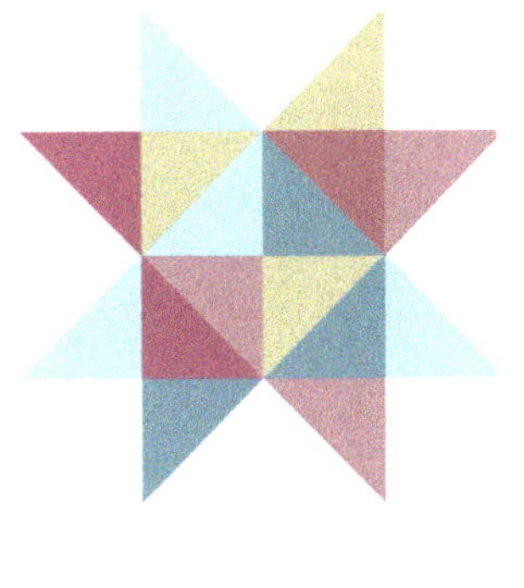

Resources

How to Print

Get Printable, full page Templates of the Curriculum Map and more! You can follow the QR Code below to view and download PDFs of all templates and outlines.

Step 1: Hold your smart phone camera up to the QR code and tap on the link that pops up.

Or you can take a picture of this page and on your smart phone then tap and hold the QR code and the link will pop up.

Step 2: Enter your Details and access will be emailed to you!

Step 3: Scroll through the list of resources and select the one you're looking for.

Step 4: Download the PDF.

Step 6: Print.

Templates and Worksheets

Find all available resources to print through a QR code at the end of this section.

Included in this Section:

Maps

- Workshop Curriculum Map
- Program Map 1
- Program Map 2

Templates:

- Digital Course Outline
- Program Outline 1
- Program Outline 2

Curriculum Map

Name of the Workshop:

Topic:

Objective:

Format: Price:

How do they demonstrate Mastery?

Curriculum Map

Description:

Curriculum Map

Use this space for Action Mapping or listing steps.

Curriculum Map

Use this space for Action Mapping or listing steps.

Curriculum Map

Use this space for Action Mapping or listing steps.

Curriculum Map

Use this space for Action Mapping or listing steps.

Curriculum Map

Student Materials

Teachers Materials

Curriculum Map

Learning Support for Students. What do they have access to for supporting their learning after the workshop?

Curriculum Map

Brainstorm

Program Map 1

Name of the Program:

Topic:

Objective (sell patterns, workshop interest, book sales, etc.)

Format

Price

Introduction (approx. 5-7 minutes):

Program Map 1

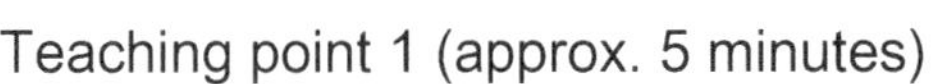

Teaching point 1 (approx. 5 minutes)

2-3 Examples that showcase teaching point 1

Teaching point 2 (approx. 5 minutes)

2-3 Examples that showcase teaching point 2

Program Map 1

Teaching point 3 (approx. 5 minutes)

2-3 Examples that showcase teaching point 3

Teaching point 4 (approx. 5 minutes)

2-3 Examples that showcase teaching point 4

Program Map 1

9-12 examples that showcase all 4 teaching points (approx. 20 minutes)

Program Map 1

Brief summary of the teaching points and how you expand on those in the follow up workshop (if applicable) (approx. 3-5 minutes)

Conclusion: how do they follow up with you? What did you bring with you to sell? (approx. 5 minutes)

Program Map 2

Name of the Program:

Topic:

Objective (sell patterns, workshop interest, book sales, etc.):

Format: Price:

Introduction (approx. 5-7 minutes):

Program Map 2

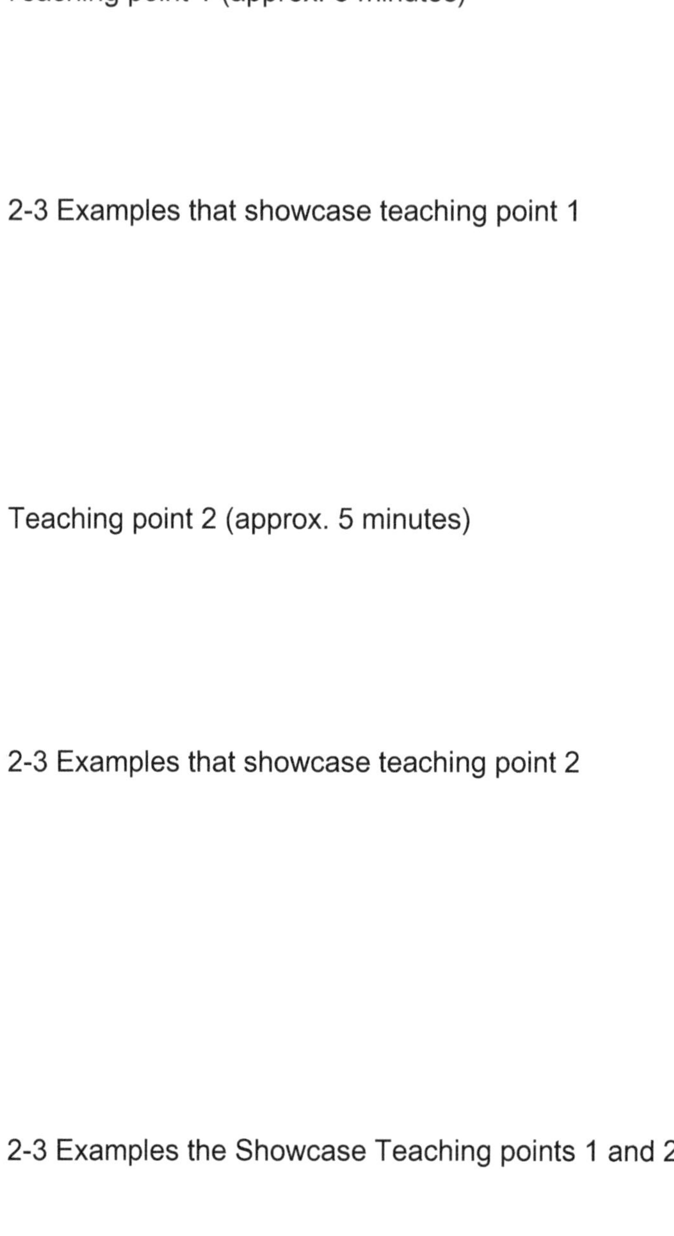

Teaching point 1 (approx. 5 minutes)

2-3 Examples that showcase teaching point 1

Teaching point 2 (approx. 5 minutes)

2-3 Examples that showcase teaching point 2

2-3 Examples the Showcase Teaching points 1 and 2

Program Map 2

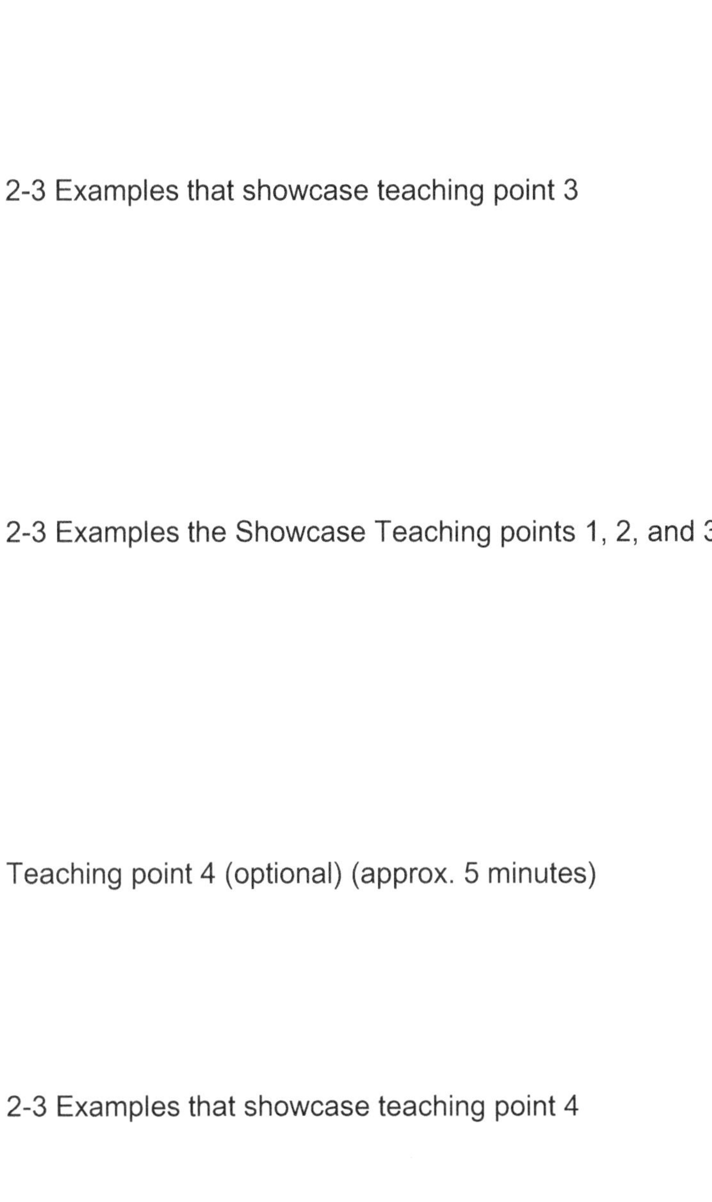

Teaching point 3 (approx. 5 minutes)

2-3 Examples that showcase teaching point 3

2-3 Examples the Showcase Teaching points 1, 2, and 3

Teaching point 4 (optional) (approx. 5 minutes)

2-3 Examples that showcase teaching point 4

Program Map 2

2-3 Examples the Showcase Teaching points 1, 2, 3, and 4

Brief summary of the teaching points and how you expand on those in the follow up workshop (if applicable) (approx. 3-5 minutes)

Program Map2

Conclusion: how do they follow up with you? What did you bring with you to sell? (approx. 5 minutes)

Digital Course Outline

This outline is ideal for a prerecorded digital course. Feel free to take creative liberty with the order and fit it to the subject your teaching. Each Module can be an Action Step with Subactions underneath. You're going to bookend your Action Steps between an Introduction and Closing Module. The amount of Middle Modules can vary depending on how many action steps are needed. Use the exercises in the Map it Out section to decide what needs to be included and what can be left out.

Course Name:

Subtitle:

Subject:

Objective:

Price:

Module 1: The Introduction:

- Introduce yourself.
- Introduce the subject and any background information they may need.
- Outline the course for your student, a visual walk through with a screen recording can be beneficial.
    - Describe how to use the software or platform the course is hosted on.
    - Demonstrate where to find resources, bonuses, community etc.
- Inform them how to contact for help or questions.

Digital Course Outline continued:

Middle Modules: The Content
Modules are organized by main actions with appropriate subactions underneath.

Each module outline should look like this:

- Main action title
- Introduction to the action.
    - Outline the subactions in this module if there's more than two subactions.
- Teach the subactions.
- Add a transition at the end for the next subaction.
- Repeat for each subaction.
- Conclude the Module by summarize the subactions and add a transition to set up the next module.

Keep all videos between approximately 3-30 minutes long. They can be longer if necessary, but 30 minutes is the goal.

Closing Module: Next Steps

- Thank them.
- Briefly summarize what they learned.
- Demonstrate how they can reuse the skill or content in their next project and share what their next steps could be.
- Ask for their feedback.
- Share how they can follow up or keep in touch with you.

Program 1 Outline

Introduction

- Share who you are, the topic you'll be presenting and let them know what your history or experience with the subject. Include any important background information they need.

Instruction

- Teaching point 1:
  - 2-3 examples that showcase teaching point 1
- Teaching point 2:
  - 2-3 examples that showcase teaching point 2
- Teaching Point 3:
  - 2-3 examples that showcase teaching point 3
- Teaching point 4:
  - 2-3 examples that showcase teaching point 4
- 9-12 examples that showcase all 4 teaching points.

Summarize Your Teaching Points

Lead a discussion or reflection (optional)

Conclusion (approx. 5 minutes):

- Share what you offer (patterns, workshops, services, etc) and ONE way to access it (this can be your website or landing page)
- Share ONE way to keep in touch with you (typically your main social media account or your email list)
- Share a little about what you've brought with you today to sell (if applicable)
- Ask for questions or invite them to speak to you after the presentation and thank the group for hosting.

Program 2 Outline

Introduction

- Share who you are, the topic you'll be presenting and let them know what your history or experience with the subject. Include any important background information they need.

Instruction

- Teaching Point 1:
  - 2-3 examples
- Teaching Point 2:
  - 2 examples of Teaching Point 2
  - 2-3 example quilts that showcase the first two teaching points
- Teaching Point 3:
  - 2 examples of Teaching Point 3
  - 2-3 example quilts that showcase the first three teaching points
- Teaching Point 4:
  - 2 examples of Teaching Point 4
  - 2-3 example quilts that showcase all teaching points

Summarize Your Teaching Points
Lead a discussion or reflection

Conclusion (approx. 5 minutes):

  - Share what you offer (patterns, workshops, services, etc) and ONE way to access it (this can be your website or landing page)
  - Share ONE way to keep in touch with you (typically your main social media account or your email list)
  - Share a little about what you've brought with you today to sell (if applicable)
  - Ask for questions or invite them to speak to you after the presentation and thank the group for hosting.

All Resources

With the Purchase of the book, *Workshops Unleashed*, you received much more than a book. Follow the QR Code below to take advantage of all the resources that come with the book:

- **Secret Meet Your Colleagues Podcast**
- **Templates and Worksheets**
- **Free *Workshops Unleashed* Community**
- **and More!**

Step 1: Hold your smart phone camera up to the QR code and tap on the link that pops up.

Or you can take a picture of this page and on your smart phone then tap and hold the QR code and the link will pop up.

Step 2: Enter your Details and access will be emailed to you!

References

"38 Arts and Crafts Industry Statistics to Know [April 2024 Update]." Scottmax.com, January 23, 2024. https://scottmax.com/arts-and-crafts-industry-statistics/.

"Arts and Crafts Market Size, Share, Growth, Global Industry Analysis, by Type (Painting and Drawing, Sewing and Fabric, Paper Crafts, Kids Crafts, Arts and Crafts Tools, and Others), by Application (Personal Use and Commercial Use), Covid-19 Impact, Latest Trends, Segmentation, Driving Factors, Restraining Factors, Key Industry Players, Regional Insights, and Forecast from 2024 to 2031." Arts and Crafts Market - 2024 To 2031 Report, April 8, 2024. https://www.businessresearchinsights.com/market-reports/arts-and-crafts-market-100197.

Bean, Cammy. *The Accidental Instructional Designer: Learning Design for the Digital Age*. Alexandria: ASTD Press, 2014.

Dirksen, Julie. *Design for How People Learn*. San Francisco: New Riders, 2016.

"Facts and Figures: Economic Empowerment." UN Women – Headquarters, February 2024. https://www.unwomen.org/en/what-we-do/economic-empowerment/facts-and-figures.

Gilbert, Elizabeth. *Big Magic: Creative Living Beyond Fear*. New York, NY: Riverhead Books, 2016.

Gordon, David, Anne Meyer, and David Rose. *Universal Design for Learning*. Peabody: CAST Professional Publishing, 2016.

Moore, Cathy. *Map it: The Hands-on Guide to Strategic Training Design*. United States: Montesa Press, 2017.

Parker, Priya. *The Art of Gathering: How we Meet and Why it Matters*. New York: Riverhead Books, 2020.

Porterfield, Amy. *Two Weeks Notice: Find the courage to quit your job, make more money, work where you want, and change the world.* Carlsbad, CA: H Business, Hay House, Inc., 2023.

Rodgers, Rachel. *We should all be millionaires: A woman's guide to earning more, building wealth, and gaining economic power.* New York, NY: HarperCollins Leadership, an imprint of HarperCollins, 2021.

"Today's Quilting Trends." Craft Industry Alliance, November 7, 2022. https://fabshopnet.com/wp-content/uploads/downloads/2022_TodaysQuiltingTrends-1.pdf.

Walker, Jeff. *Launch (updated & expanded edition): How to sell almost anything online, build a business you love, and live the life of your dreams.* Hay House Business, 2021.

Woodard, Monique. "Unlocking the Trillion-Dollar Female Economy." TechCrunch, May 22, 2023. https://techcrunch.com/2023/05/21/unlocking-the-trillion-dollar-female-economy/.

About the Author

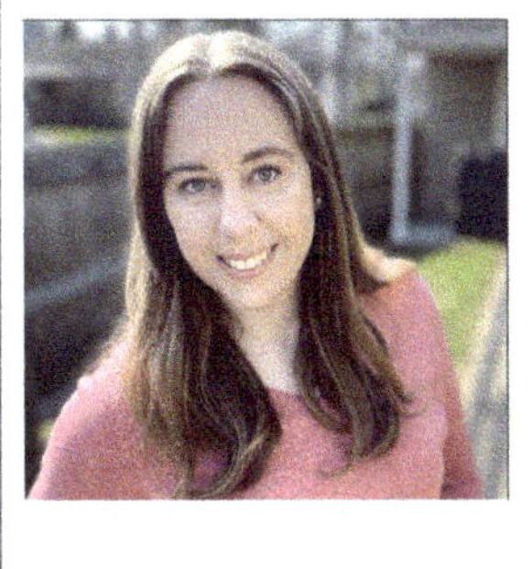

I began designing and publishing quilt patterns and teaching quilting workshops as a way to afford my daily Starbucks. As I discovered how enjoyable and profitable it could be, I became fully immersed! Combining my passion for quilting with my profession as an Instructional Designer and a Master of Education, I founded the *Quilt Patch Course Academy* and wrote *Workshops Unleashed.*

I assist quilt and creative teachers in transforming their craft into a successful course or workshop that is both lucrative and impactful. As a teacher, coach, and author, my goal is to help you create engaging and impactful workshops that keep students coming back for more!

More From Tori!

Tune in to *Quilting on the Side* Podcast with Tori and Andi!

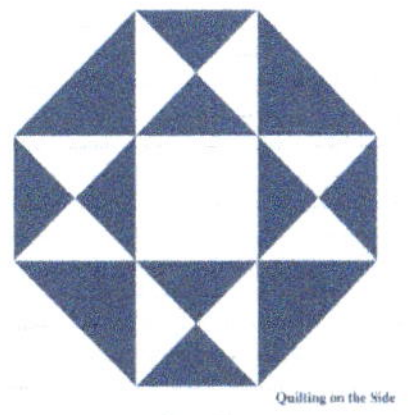

Quilting on the Side is the podcast that weaves together the art of quilting and the pursuit of a profitable side business. Join co-hosts Tori and Andi as they delve into the world of quilt pattern design, course creation, and digital marketing, guiding you on a journey to turn your favorite hobby into a money-making venture.

Workshops Unleashed: The Course is coming soon!

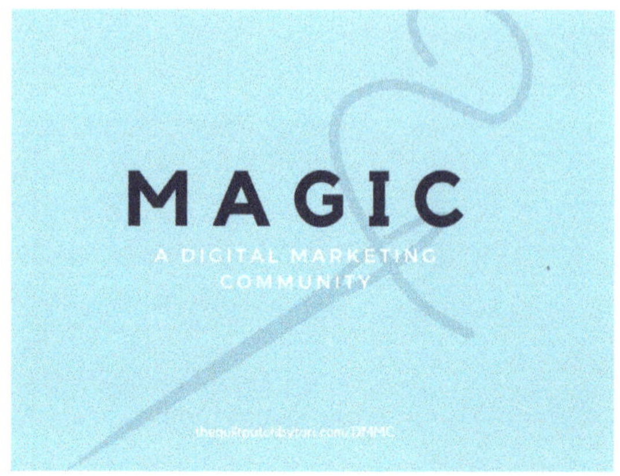

Digital Marketing Help: Join the Digital Marketing Magic Community and Program (DMMC)

Tori McElwain founded and designed the program for the Digital Marketing Magic Community and Program (DMMC). See more at TheQuiltPatchbyTori.com.

See more about the DMMC

Other books by Tori McElwain:

What the FPP is That? Quilting Terms: A Vernacular Guide

Quilter's Notebook Series available on Amazon

Acknowledgments

This book is a dream come true and would not have happened without a strong team behind me.

To my sister, Tisha, you've been my first reader, toughest critic, and biggest supporter from the beginning. From grade school essays to college papers, and now this book, you've always been there—ready with an eye roll, a late-night study session, and countless "I think you mean this" or "quick, write that down!" I wouldn't have dared to dream this big without your unwavering belief in me. Your support has meant the world to me, and this book is as much yours as it is mine. Thank you for always being by my side.

To my spouse, Ryan, your love and support have been the foundation of this journey. Thank you for stepping up in every way—watching the kids, cooking meals, and gently insisting that I get some rest when I wanted to keep working late into the night. Your belief in me and your willingness to shoulder extra responsibilities allowed me to pour my heart into this book. I couldn't have done this without you, and I'm endlessly grateful for your partnership and encouragement every step of the way.

Special Thanks

A huge thank you to Darla Hall whose exquisite quilted samples are included in this book. Her beautiful work has made everything look even better and really brought the pages to life. I'm so grateful she let me share her amazing quilts with us. Darla's artistry is truly inspiring. If you want to learn from her, be sure to check out QuiltingWithDarla.com.

To Melissa Strange: Words cannot express my gratitude for your unwavering support throughout the creation of *Workshops Unleashed*. Your sharp insights, creative brilliance, and constant encouragement pushed me to new heights. You kept me on track, stretched my thinking, and transformed my dyslexic scribbles into something truly meaningful. This book wouldn't be what it is without your dedication and belief in me. Thank you for helping me bring this vision to life.

If you're looking for a content editor:

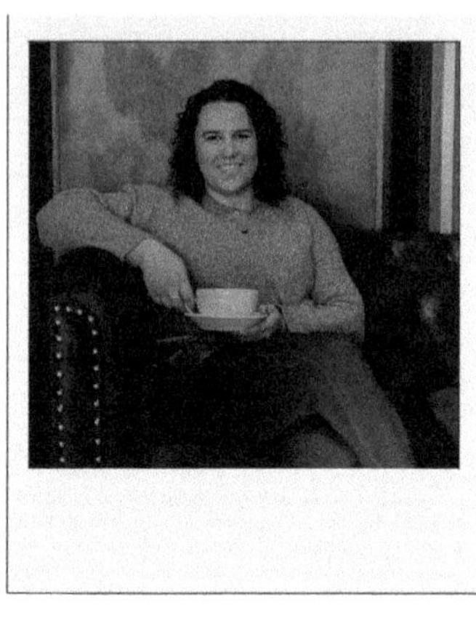

Melissa Strange | Editor & Proofreader at topshelfproofreading.com

Melissa's passion for the written word is evident in every project she undertakes. With a rich background in language arts—from earning a degree in English to teaching English as a second language—she honed her deep understanding of language mechanics, which she now brings to her work in the editing field. Her journey into professional proofreading was fueled by her love of literature and a desire to help authors refine their work to its fullest potential.

Melissa is not only deeply committed to supporting authors through the often challenging process of preparing their work for publication but also to supporting military spouses and families, as she is deeply immersed in the community. Melissa is the daughter of a retired Naval Officer and the wife of a Senior Enlisted Airman for fourteen years and recognizes the value of a strong, supportive network in helping military families navigate their unique challenges.

Melissa takes great care to ensure that every manuscript she works on is not only free of errors but also polished and cohesive, allowing the author's voice to shine through. Her work on this book is yet another example of her devotion to helping authors achieve their best work, making her an invaluable partner in the creative process.

More Info

The Quilt Pattern on the cover is *Follow the Stars*. It was designed, pieced, and quilted by Tori McElwain of *The Quilt Patch by Tori.*

The cover photo was taken by Sarah Hall. You can find her at hallsarah688@gmail.com for photography or graphic design inquiries. All other pictures in the book were taken by Tori McElwain or by a friend of Tori McElwain with Tori's phone.

The *Meet Your Colleagues Podcast* was edited by Devan Robinson.

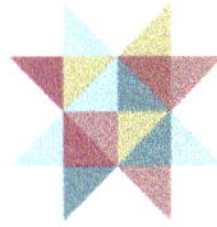

The awesome star that is the central branding of the book was designed by Kathleen Fritzsche!

Thank you!

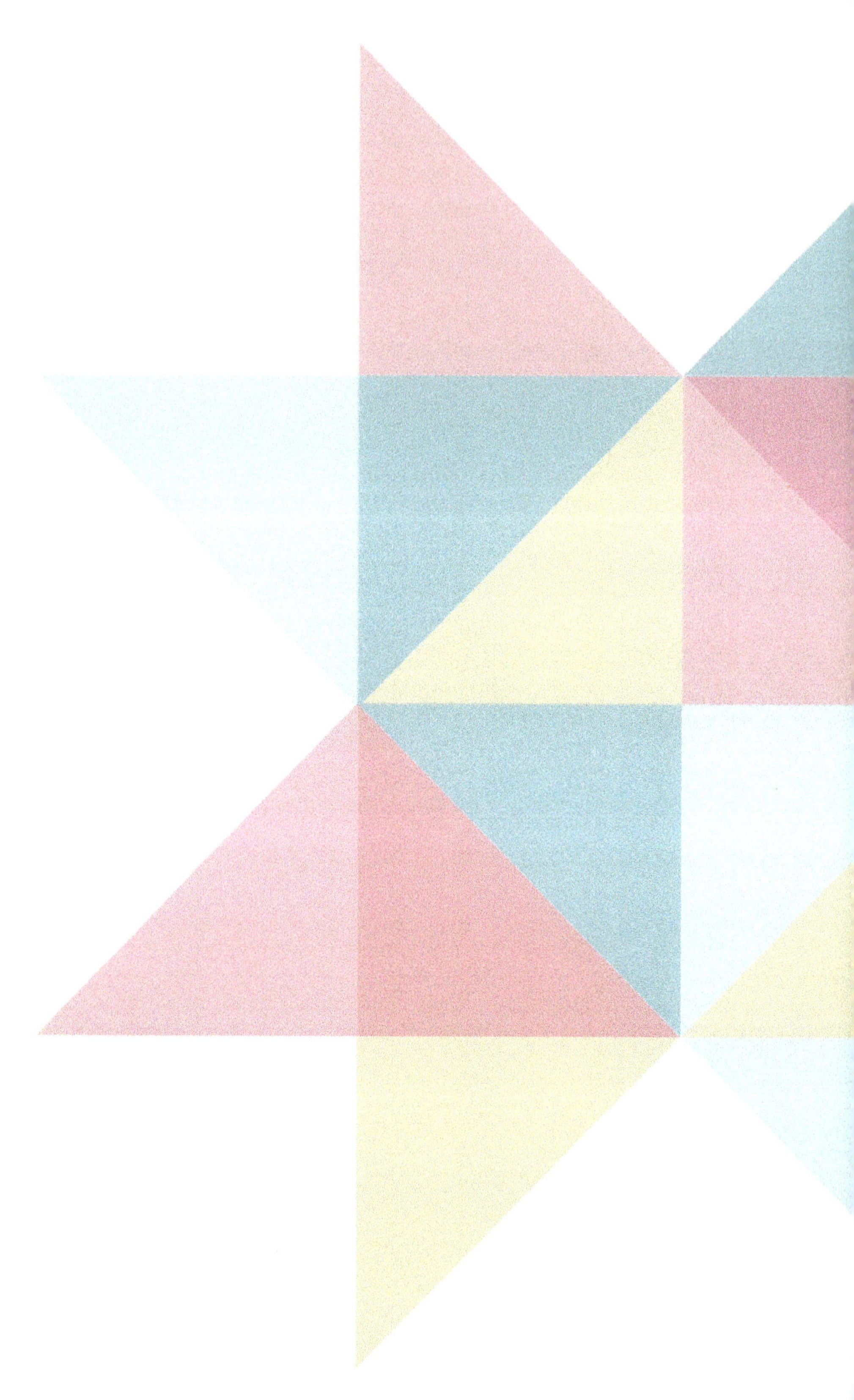

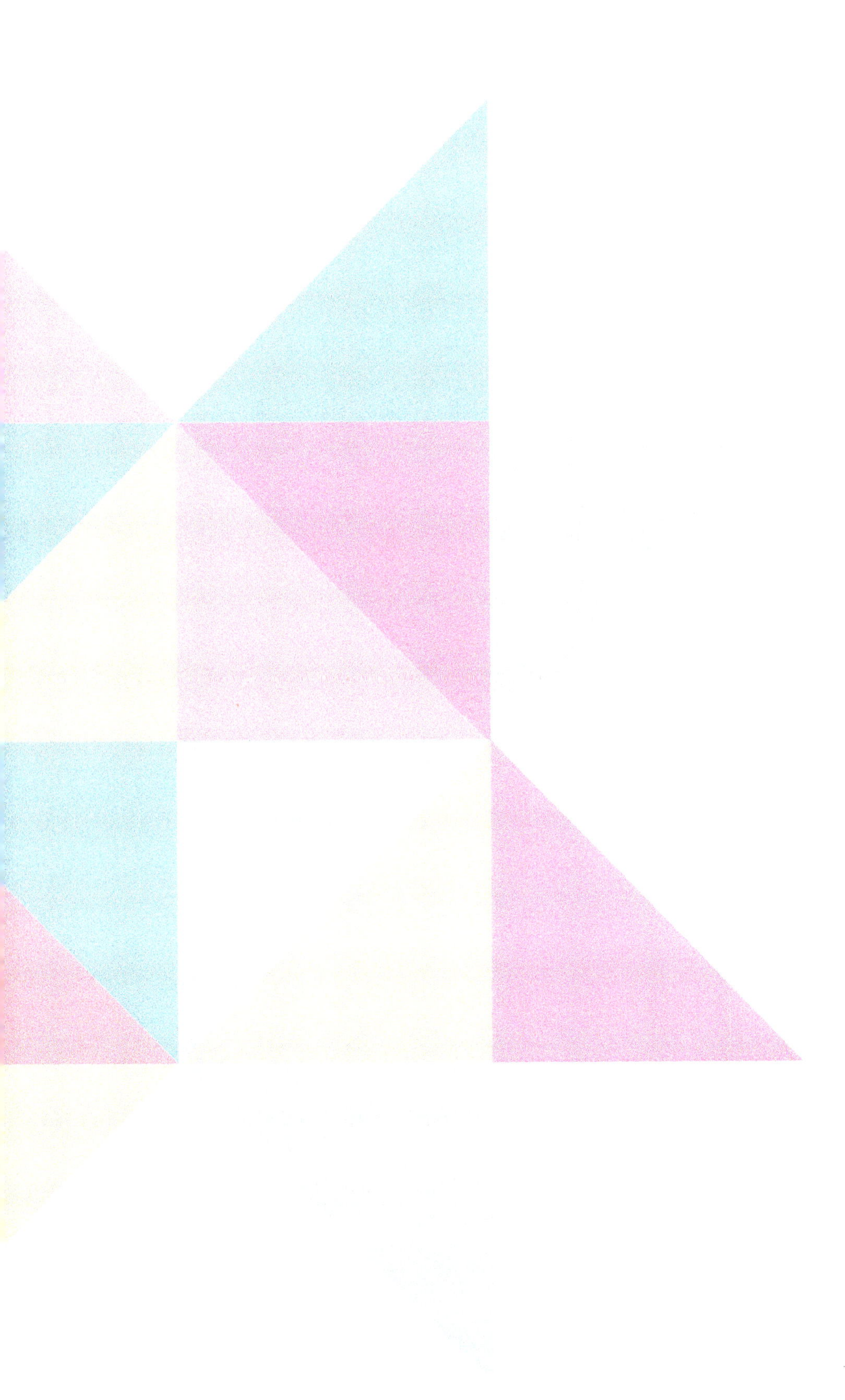

www.ingramcontent.com/pod-product-compliance
Ingram Content Group UK Ltd.
Pitfield, Milton Keynes, MK11 3LW, UK
UKHW062302290726
14090UKWH00017B/841